Essential Measures for Student Success

Implementing Cooperation, Collaboration, and Coordination Between Schools and Parents

Edwena Kirby

ROWMAN & LITTLEFIELD EDUCATION
A division of
ROWMAN & LITTLEFIELD PUBLISHERS, INC.
Lanham • New York • Toronto • Plymouth, UK

Published by Rowman & Littlefield Education
A division of Rowman & Littlefield Publishers, Inc.
A wholly owned subsidiary of The Rowman & Littlefield Publishing Group, Inc.
4501 Forbes Boulevard, Suite 200, Lanham, Maryland 20706
http://www.rowmaneducation.com

Estover Road, Plymouth PL6 7PY, United Kingdom

Copyright © 2012 by Edwena Kirby

All rights reserved. No part of this book may be reproduced in any form or by any electronic or mechanical means, including information storage and retrieval systems, without written permission from the publisher, except by a reviewer who may quote passages in a review.

British Library Cataloguing in Publication Information Available

Library of Congress Cataloging-in-Publication Data

Kirby, Edwena, 1953-
Essential measures for student success : implementing cooperation, collaboration, and coordination between schools and parents / Edwena Kirby.
  p. cm.
Includes bibliographical references and index.
ISBN 978-1-61048-759-7 (cloth : alk. paper) -- ISBN 978-1-61048-760-3 (pbk. : alk. paper) -- ISBN 978-1-61048-761-0 (electronic)
 1. School improvement programs--United States. 2. Education--Parent participation--United States. 3. Education--Aims and objectives--United States. I. Title.
  LB2822.82.K523 2012
  371.200973--dc23
                                                                2011051120

The paper used in this publication meets the minimum requirements of American National Standard for Information Sciences Permanence of Paper for Printed Library Materials, ANSI/NISO Z39.48-1992.

Printed in the United States of America

contents

Preface	vii
Acknowledgments	ix
Introduction	xi
Part I: Factors Impacting Student Achievement	**1**
1 The Historical Mission of Education	3
2 Children in Your School	7
3 Understanding Child Development	11
4 Systems Impacting the Lives of Children	17
5 Ecological Factors Influencing the Behavior of Children	21
Part II: Strategies for Closing the Achievement Gap	**41**
6 Children's Responses to Their School Experience	45
7 Love	51
8 Power	63
9 Fun	71
10 Freedom	77
11 Success for All	81
Appendix	89
About the Author	91

Preface

As a school social worker, a plethora of opportunities has existed for personal observations and one-on-one experiences of both at-risk and low-performing students. Contacts through conducting home visitations, completing educational assessments, coordinating parental involvement, mentoring, monitoring attendance and truancy, developing and implementing student behavioral programs and contracts, and providing individual, group, and therapeutic counseling allowed dialogue with students and their parents.

Those encounters afforded rich experiences in understanding students' needs and their desires. More importantly, their needs were identified directly from the source. Strategies and approaches that worked and those that did not work were observed.

On a personal level, additional knowledge of what helps African-American students achieve academically was acquired through the author's own child's challenges, which will be shared, as well as some concerns that were consistently verbalized by students of various ethnicities, across grade levels, regarding their educational experiences.

Given this, as an educator and a parent, there is great concern about the gap in achievement of children, particularly African Americans. Their long history of poor academic performance is a problem as well as the fact that their overall achievement lags significantly behind that of European-American children. Even today, when comparing European-American children's achievement with that of African-American children and other ethnic groups, a major gap continues to exist.

It appears that some of the same unsuccessful practices are being implemented over and over again that claim to "leave no child behind." In schools there is a consistent pattern of not recognizing or considering what children display daily in their behavior is indicative of their needs. Educators must recognize that children's needs must be met first before they can perform to their level of potential.

To close the achievement gap, educators cannot afford to allow insurmountable challenges, barriers, and obstacles to deter them from continuing their efforts. They must begin by examining, redefining, and/or reevaluating their beliefs, attitudes, and practices regarding the most vulnerable and precious treasures parents have placed in their care.

They must acknowledge that all children or students (which will be used interchangeably in this book), especially those who are academically underachieving, must be educated in a manner that addresses their learning style. And to teach them any other way perpetuates an achievement gap.

Furthermore, educators must recognize that for some children, traditional school, as we know it, does not best meet their academic needs. Other school options must be available such as vocational training programs, technology training programs, and/or entrepreneurship training programs. In addition, as the needs of children have become more complex, therapeutic programs must be available.

This book does not claim to be a "magic wand," rectifying all concerns related to closing the achievement gap. It merely embraces what is known about human development and human behavior that can positively impact student achievement. It highlights that change must be welcomed by all who serve children. It emphasizes that there must be cooperation, collaboration, and coordination between schools and parents.

The intent of this book is to serve as a resource for administrators, teachers, and parents, providing some practical strategies whereby their efforts will result in improving the achievement level of children. The hope is that this book will help educators and parents look more closely at some simple measures they can take to improve children's academic success.

Acknowledgments

I am most grateful to God, who is my source of support in all matters of life. To all, especially students and their parents whom I have served over the past thirty years in the field of social work, this book would not be possible without you. Thanks for the rich experiences and the opportunities to serve you.

Deneen and Arnita, thanks for your contribution. Your suggestions and comments were appreciated. Again, thanks.

Introduction

"Skill to do comes of doing."
—Ralph Emerson

When it comes to educating children, why is it educators omit applying what they know? They know that family has been widely accepted as being important to children. In addition, they know that peers have been considered significant in the lives of children. With this long history of awareness, it would be reasonable that they would consistently use the strongest forces in the lives of children to influence them to excel academically.

Educators should not ignore that for many decades data have widely documented that early development of children is shaped by their family and that social development of children is influenced through peer relations.[1] These findings should compel them to seek the involvement of parents and peers in an effort to close the achievement gap.

As another resource, in an effort to enhance the intellectual development of children, the community must be sought. Educators must recognize that churches and organizations have played a pivotal role in providing guidance and financial assistance to children. In fact, parents often use community organizations because of their interest in children.

To help improve the academic performance of students, educators must not allow the two questions they often ask guide them in how they assist students: "Do all parents want their child/children to be successful?" and "Do all children want to be successful?" To both questions, the answer is yes. Without debate, there is not a parent who wants his or her child to be a failure. Likewise, no child aspires to be unsuccessful. Therefore, with complete confidence, it can be boldly stated, "success" is the hope of parents and children.

When we define success we must recognize that it may have one meaning for one person and another meaning for another person. For some individuals, how to be successful may not be completely clear. Guidance may increase the possibility of success. Then, in some instances, hope of success may only be experienced because no support or resource is believed to be available.

Among many African-American students, despite their desire to succeed, the gap in achievement poses the likelihood of a dismal future, leading often to high dropout rates, unemployment, and crime. To increase the possibility of a productive life for them and all students, educators must take measures to decrease the gap in achievement. They must develop an attitude of "no fault, consensus, and collaboration," eradicating blame and agreeing on ways, as a team, to solve problems and concerns that affect the academic growth of all children.[2]

To close the achievement gap, this book advocates using the "Hook" (love, power, fun, and freedom) as a strategy, which is explained through Urie Bronfenbrenner's ecological model. Part I of this book focuses on the factors impacting student achievement. The first chapter explains the historical mission of education. Chapter 2 describes children in your school. Chapter 3 presents an understanding of child development.

Chapter 4 identifies the systems impacting the lives of children. Chapter 5 describes the ecological factors influencing the behavior of children. Chapter 6 reports children's responses to their school experience. Part II provides strategies for closing the achievement gap. It offers a succinct understanding of a strategy called the "Hook" and explains how the "Hook" will help close the achievement gap.

Chapter 7 defines the first feature of the "Hook," love. Chapter 8 describes the second feature of the "Hook," power. Chapter 9 explains the third feature of the "Hook," fun. Chapter 10 defines the final feature of the "Hook," freedom. Chapter 11 presents a "win-win" situation for students, educators, and parents, which translates into success for all.

NOTES

1. J. W. V. Zanden, *Human development*, Rev. ed. (New York: McGraw-Hill, 2000).
2. J. Comer, et al., child by Child (New York: 1999).

Part I

Factors Impacting Student Achievement

Chapter One

The Historical Mission of Education

"We cannot stand still or slip backwards. We must go forward now together."
—Gerald Ford

The intent of education in the United States historically has been to serve as the gateway to social mobility and career development.[1] As early as the 1800s, mass education was a goal.[2] In 1850, half of the United States population between the ages of five and nineteen was enrolled in school.

By 1918, a mandatory education law was imposed that required children in every state to attend school until age sixteen or completion of the eighth grade. The mandatory education law forced many children, particularly African Americans, to leave farms and factories to enroll in school.[3] Today, throughout the country, the focus of schools is to meet the academic needs of all children. Schools must promote the development of all children. And they must be child centered.

The mission of schools is to promote the intellectual levels of competency of all children, aiming for higher academic performance and test scores, and thus expanding future possibilities and occupational choices.[4] The plan is that every child will have the opportunity to experience success and be productive.

THE UNEXPECTED AND UNPLANNED OUTCOME

Although an aim, evaluations and assessments show that some children have not made sufficient academic growth. Deficits are reflected in their achievement level, especially among African-American children, who often live in an environment that is physically, emotionally, socially, and intellectually stressful.[5] Their poor performance has warranted much assistance.

Schools have attempted for decades to address this problem by offering information, experiences, opportunities, facts, and ideas that would provide a productive future for all children, yet inadequate success continues to be reported. Many children, despite their efforts, continue to experience school failure, and educators commonly see this lack of success during early child development extending into adulthood.

Children seem to be unaware of their own identity and the identity of others. It appears that they do not recognize their talents, strengths, or weaknesses that would promote their growth and development. The confusion they display tends to cause problems at home as well as at school.

One explanation that studies reveal is that children encounter socialized, culturally approved gender roles wherein females are encouraged in areas of arts, humanities, and social sciences while males are advised to major in economics, engineering, computer science, and natural science. Another explanation provided is that the culture values that schools impart and have practiced for many years cause some children to become unmotivated. Their practices and introductions of "showcases" of success contribute to the unproductiveness of some children.[6]

School-sponsored activities of competition such as spelling contests and athletic activities highlight the success of some children as they illuminate the failure of others. Although unintentionally, these activities cause some children to appear to be slow. Some children consider these forms of culture value experiences positive while others, especially deprived children, who are often African Americans, find these experiences demeaning.

Deprived children are clearly at a disadvantage prior to being placed in a competitive situation. They are reluctant to risk further failure when they have experienced years of school failure. In fact, they will generally do whatever is necessary to avoid future failure.

Formal regimentation is another aspect of school that creates difficulty for some children. Their first experience is often in a school setting, especially among African-American children. While the intent of formal regimentation is to introduce time frames required for future experiences, adjustment to structure and change, such as routines and schedules, presents a problem for some children.

For educators, this means it is important to develop a school environment that is not physically, emotionally, socially, and intellectually stressful to prevent children from having additional difficulty adjusting to structure. Cooperation, collaboration, and coordination are important in order to accomplish this. Teachers must not overlook that a plethora of studies have widely documented the first year of school as the foundation that highly impacts achievement.

When children start school, they begin with similar achievement and test scores, but by the end of their first year, African-American children's performance lags significantly behind that of European-American children's. In fact, during the second year of school, the gap widens.[7] Poor grades cause many students to become disinterested in school.

Similar to this, in a study of rural communities it was reported that their school environment rarely promotes healthy development or intellectual growth of some children. The reason offered was that some teachers spend more time covering curriculum content than attending to specific academic needs of children who fall behind. Children's developmental needs involving school projects, music, physical education activities, and spontaneous play were frequently ignored. Teachers were too focused on attempting to establish authority and classroom climate.[8]

In that same study it was found that in rural communities, children received an inferior education in troubled public school systems than their counterparts in less-rural settings. Some teachers were oblivious that essential to children are teacher traits such as smiles and praises, which encourage adaptability, flexibility, and enthusiasm for learning. If they employed these forms of constructive teacher mannerisms, they would see improvement in children's motivation and desire to learn.[9]

SUMMARY

Students' academic performance will improve when teachers take simple measures. Teachers must be willing to change the way students view the classroom environment. This change entails helping children experience a sense of being valued and accepted, thus creating an environment conducive to learning.

Teachers must not assume that all children have experienced structure and routines. Those who have not must be exposed and taught. The skills that they learn must become part of their daily routines. As teachers discover students' talents and strengths, they must find ways to help students experience success so that they will be motivated to learn.

Academic growth of students will manifest when teachers align their teaching styles with the strengths, the talents, and the abilities of students. Furthermore, effective teacher mannerisms will increase the academic achievement of children who have had a long history of poor performance. Student academic growth will further heighten when teachers increase their expectations rather than reduce them.

Based on income, teachers must never assume that parents of low socioeconomic status are uninterested in helping their children. More effort, rather than less effort, should be exerted to communicate with these parents because the status of disadvantage is often an indicator of lower performance. Given this, regular contact with these parents will likely increase the level of their children's academic performance.

NOTES

1. A. Pinkey, *Black Americans* (Englewood Cliffs, NJ: Prentice-Hall, 1969).
2. J.Q. Wilson, *The marriage problem: How our culture has weakened families* (New York: Harper Collins, 2002).
3. J. J. Macionis, Society: *The basics*, Rev. ed. (Upper Saddle River, NJ: Prentice-Hall, 1996).
4. C. Lim, H. S. Adelman, "Establishing school-based, collaborative teams to coordinate resources: A case study," *Social Work in Education* 19, no.4 (October, 1997):266-76.
5. R. F. Biehler, J. Snowman, *Psychology applied to teaching*, Rev. ed. (Boston: Houghton Mifflin, 1993).
6. R.E. Anderson, I. Carter, G. P Lowe, *Human behavior in the social environment: A social systems* (New York: Aldine De Gruyter, 1999), 5.
7. S. Danziger, A. C. Lin, "Coping with poverty: The social contexts of neighborhood, work and family in the African American community," *Perspectives* 6, no.3 (2000): 41-46.
8. D. J. Palmer, "Preparation and experience of elementary teachers to work with community services for at-risk children. *Education* 121, no.3, (2001):554-65.
9. F. Vitaro, D. Larocque, R. E. Tremblay, "Negative social experiences and dropping out of school," *Educational Psychology* 21, no.4, (2001): 401-15.

Chapter Two

Children in Your School

"Truthfulness is a cornerstone in character, and if it be not firmly laid in youth, there will ever after be a weak spot in the foundation."
—Jefferson Davis

School is the place that guides the life path of students. It is the place where students expect to receive help in their learning. They enter school with ambivalent feelings. Some are anxious. Some are happy. And some are sad. To expand our frame of thinking regarding the students we serve, we must acknowledge that:

- Students are different in many ways, including race, gender, religion, and political orientation.
- Their economic backgrounds differ.
- Some are wealthy.
- Some are poor.
- Some come from low- to medium-income households.
- Some will work hard.
- Some will do enough to pass their grade.
- Some will do very little and sometimes nothing at all.

Often major achievement deficits are prevalent among problematic students and others who are affected by their actions: after leaving home, a student gets off the bus or comes into the school and goes to the cafeteria for breakfast. As the tardy bell rings, she slowly makes her way to the classroom. She puts her head on the desk. Don't you dare bother her! In the locker room, she teases, pushes, and threatens other girls.

And he makes multiple trips to the trash can, distracting other students each time. In his attempts to get a response, he causes altercations in the classroom. He is disrespectful and noncompliant. If he does his homework, he rarely completes it.

Nearly every day, some of the same students are tardy. Do they even have a place to stay? Perhaps they are sleeping under a bridge or in a car. Can they make significant changes in their home environment or family functioning?

Is substance abuse a problem in their home? Are they witnessing domestic violence? Are they, themselves, victims of abuse?

Do they have critically ill parents or grandparents in the home? Are they, themselves, managing the home? Do they have to work a job in order to have food to eat or help maintain the household?

Are these students staying up late each night? Do they eat breakfast before coming to school? Did they take a bath the night before or the morning of? With little to no help from the absent father, the mother is likely doing the best she can. In those situations where the father is the primary caregiver, he too is likely providing to the best of his ability.

Could the reason these children have a hygiene problem perhaps be that they have no water or electricity in their homes? If you travel in their neighborhood you will see that they spend more time outside than inside. They are attempting to escape the bitter coldness of their homes. Outside is warmer, and it allows them to inhale fresh air instead of stale, offensive odors from their malnourished, inadequately groomed pets (dogs, cats, goats, chickens, parrots, hamsters, etc.).

The plight of some children in your school is unimaginable, and perhaps you are unaware that some live in poor housing conditions wherein they do not have flooring, except the dry earth or red clay. Often cockroaches crawl about their kitchen tables and walls. Each night, they sleep on a hard floor because their parents do not have adequate money to purchase a bed or other furnishings due to other financial obligations.

The much-needed medical attention is not sought or received due to insufficient funds for copayments or transportation to a medical facility. Their substandard housing conditions may mean that they have to use a five-gallon bucket as a toilet. Their plumbing is inoperable. Their roof is leaking. And their house is infested with rats.

These are the children who often come to school unready to learn. They do not have paper and pencils. To expect them to think about their school assignments when their home environment does not meet their basic needs or provide nurturing that enables them to be productive is unrealistic.

Frequently, in these and other students, developmental delays in physical, cognitive, and social skills are prevalent. Some of these students are slow in developing proper motor skills. Others show deficits in their ability to comprehend or problem-solve. And some refuse to interact with other children because they do not know how, which causes them to become rejected children.

These and many other difficult challenges are what children in your school encounter, which are often unknown to teachers. Those who are privy to such information seldom take the time to assist in getting the social developmental needs of the students met. As such, these children's academic performance is inferior to those children who excel. Being a high achiever, she works hard at school. She completes all her assignments. She stays on task. She follows all the rules. Her peers call her a "nerd." It is okay; she has high self-esteem.

Similarly, he is eager to learn. He is always respectful and courteous. He is admired by his peers. Wearing designer shirts, jeans, and shoes, all the girls like him and say he is "buff."

SUMMARY

There are many reasons why some children's achievement level is low. Their home situation often impacts their ability to perform. How they are received at school also affects their ability to achieve.

Seldom do teachers know about the numerous challenges children face at home. They do not know about the underlying problems of students. In addition, they do not know about the struggles of their students' parents. What they do know is that during tough times, a little compassion and understanding go a long way.

This is not to imply that teachers are expected to assume the role of parents. This simply means that teachers need to offer support to their students. They need to coordinate, collaborate, and cooperate with parents.

Teachers must recognize that students want genuine care and that when it is shown, it motivates them. It builds strength in them. And it increases students' interest in learning.

Chapter Three

Understanding Child Development

"In praising or loving a child, we love and praise not that which is, but that which we hope for."
—Johann von Goethe

Effective educators and professionals must be skillful in the art of "reading" the situations that they manage. As they attempt to serve children, they must determine how to best educate them. One-sided insight will not work. The starting point is understanding child development.

The developmental needs of children must first be considered in every decision made by educators. Children's developmental needs must be the focal point of every plan developed for addressing their academic performance. Even when schools establish policies and practices, they should consider students' developmental needs.

In their effort to meet the developmental needs of children, it is important for educators to remember that human development impacts human behavior. This has been best underscored by renowned theorists Erik Erikson and Jean Piaget, who have provided some insight as to why children behave as they do. The foundation of their work captures the development of children and how their environment influences their behavior.

Erikson's extensive study of psychosocial development found that the environment of children greatly actuates their lives. The social context of their environment influences their behavior. Comparatively, Piaget's study of cognitive development emphasized that normal development occurs in an orderly and sequential manner. His assessment revealed that various changes occur in the human thought process.

From their work, they concluded that human development comprises several stages, which afford parents the opportunity to engage their children in a variety of skills that can help promote a productive life. Erikson found that the development of children is influenced as they learn from their experiences within the environment. Similarly, Piaget's observation highlighted that when children move from one stage to another, actively exploring the environment, their development is shaped.

DEVELOPMENTAL DOMAINS

The framework that Piaget and Erikson used to study human development includes three fundamental domains: physical development, cognitive development, and social development. Physical development refers to changes in the body such as height and weight, bone and muscle, and the development of the heart, the brain, and neurological features that affect motor skills. These changes in the body will occur in normal progression with a healthy individual, particularly one who receives proper nutrition, exercise, and adequate health care.[1]

Cognitive development entails changes in the mental activities of an individual such as perception, memory, reasoning, thought, and language. Cognitive skills include problem solving, interpreting, and organizing information.[2] As an individual acquires these skills, he or she will be able to actively construct his or her cognitive world and connect one idea to another. The new information that is incorporated into the existing knowledge will produce the process called "assimilation."

Assimilation allows relationships to establish through matching the cognitive structure with the physical environment. Within every experience of an individual, assimilation and accommodation are embedded. Accommodation involves adjusting new information retrieved from the environment to derive meaning of an aspect. Retrieval begins from the sensory or perceptual process called memory, which includes storing and interpreting information.

The final domain, psychosocial development, refers to changes in personality, emotions, and relationships with others. In this domain, individuals learn how to relate to others in their environment. They acquire social skills that provide them a strong foundation for later life.[3]

STAGES OF HUMAN DEVELOPMENT

Beginning in the early stages of human development, relationships emerge as emotional attachment is formed with a significant person, typically the mother. As attachment develops, the individual acquires a sense of security that encourages him or her to explore his or her environment. Within the environment, individuals are expected to be engaged in varied experiences that will shape their development.

Erikson defines the eight stages of psychosocial development as following:

- Trust versus mistrust
- Autonomy versus shame
- Initiative versus guilt
- Industry versus inferiority
- Identity versus role confusion
- Intimacy versus isolation
- Generativity versus stagnation
- Integrity versus despair

These stages are paralleled with Piaget's cognitive developmental stages, which include:

- Sensorimotor
- Preoperational
- Concrete operational
- Formal operational

The Stage of Birth to Infancy

During this stage children experience trust versus mistrust. Their sense of trust and a level of physical comfort are gained when they learn that others care. It is important for them to know that others can be trusted as well as to have their basic needs satisfied. Their sensorimotor skills, which involve only motor actions and no thinking, help them adjust to their environment.[4] This adjustment is facilitated through the actions of others.[5]

The Stage of Late Infancy

Toddlers, ages one and two, confront autonomy versus shame and doubt. They establish a will of their own. If punished too severely, a sense of shame and doubt emerges. Their preoperational skills are formed, such as the development of words, images, and drawings of the world. They begin to understand the permanence of objects and can classify and place them in groups of similarities.

The Stage of Early Childhood

The ages from two to six of early childhood mark when children encounter initiative versus guilt. They are expected to assume more responsibility for their behavior. If made to feel too anxious, uncomfortable guilt may emerge. This concrete operational period is when they are able to perform mathematical operations and engage in logical reasoning. They understand categories and groupings, relationships, measurements, and hierarchical structures.

The Stage of Middle Childhood

During elementary and middle school, children from six to twelve years experience industry versus inferiority. This more than any other time is when children are enthusiastic. They approach learning with excitement until feelings of incompetence and unproductivity emerge. During this formal operational period, children from elementary and middle school to late adulthood develop concrete thoughts that afford them the ability to think in abstract and more logical terms.[6] They entertain possibilities for the future and think in more systematic ways regarding problem solving.

The Stage of Adolescence

The period of adolescence, ages twelve to eighteen, is when identity versus confusion manifests and puberty reigns. Children encounter many new roles, causing them to seek to discover who they are and where they are going in life. If identity is shoved on them during this stage, confusion develops. Critical-thinking skills are emerging, which will allow them to forge into adulthood.

The Stage of Early Adulthood

Intimacy versus isolation impacts relationship building. Without the establishment of healthy friendships and intimate relationships, isolation will befall. The individual seeks to find self, yet lose self to another person. He or she entertains possibilities influencing his or her future.

The Stage of Middle Adulthood

Generativity versus stagnation is the period when individuals assist the next generation or become stagnant. For some individuals, at midlife, helping grandchildren creates joy. For others, the focus may be physical and intellectual changes that will benefit the next generation. They think analytically and ponder possibilities of the future.

The Stage of Late Adulthood

In the final stage, integrity versus despair, individuals recapture previous years of life and evaluate what has been accomplished. After assessment of prior life experiences, they may develop a sense of satisfaction or succumb to retrospective glances with gloom and despair. Favorable outcomes of the individuals will generate a positive outlook, while negative outcomes will cause feelings of dismay. However, as they contemplate their future goals, they will think in more logical terms.[7]

SUMMARY

If educators acknowledge these stages of human development, then they must use them as explanations to help them understand some behaviors of students within their school environment. At every level, including elementary, middle, and high school, students' physical, cognitive, and social needs must be addressed.

Physically, students need to be engaged in activities supporting motor skill development. Cognitively, students need to experience activities that will allow them to assimilate and accommodate that which has been taught. And socially, students need encounters with others that will help them build strong, healthy relationships.

Based on this, educators, "Can you honestly say that within the past year, you have considered the developmental needs of the children with whom you interact? Do you even know much about your students before attempting to teach them?" Imagine doing something different to get a different response. This would be called "change."

Change, from the vantage point of students, has the full image of what I call the "Hook," which is a strategy that will be discussed in part II of this book. It considers students' cognitive skills. It acknowledges their physical needs. And it recognizes their social developmental needs.

In your work with students, this simply means implementing a new approach to how you address their cognitive needs. You must develop different techniques to meet their physical needs. Then you must allow them to interact responsibly.

NOTES

1. J. W. Santrock, *Children* (Madison, WI: Brown & Benchmark, 1993).

2. J. Helper, "Social development of peers: The role of peers," *Social Work in Education*, 19 no.4, (1997): 243-54.
3. D. Durell, *Critical years* (Oakland CA: New Harbinger Publications, 1984).
4. B. R. Hergenhahn, M.H. Olson, *An introduction to the theories of learning*, Rev. ed. (Upper Saddle River, NJ: Prentice Hall, Inc., 1997).
J. E. Ormond, *Educational psychology: Principles and applications* (Englewood Cliffs, NJ: Prentice Hall, Inc., 1995).
6. M. Popkin, *Active parenting* (San Franciso: Harper Publishing, 1987).
7. J. W. V. Zanden, *Human development* Rev. ed. (New York: McGraw- Hill, 2000)

Chapter Four

Systems Impacting the Lives of Children

"People tend to develop a sense of injustice when various societal conditions negatively influence their family life."
—Edwena Kirby

The lives of children are impacted by various systems in society. Children do not have the ability to control how these systems affect their lives. They look to others to protect and guide them.

One way to explain this is Urie Bronfenbrenner's theoretical model. His work presents significant explanations as to how systems impact the behavior of children. His model helps us to unravel and understand some of the factors that adversely affect the lives of children. It examines several components within the environment, such as family, peers, community, and school. Finally, it offers ways to better understand how these factors impact the lives of children.

Bronfenbrenner found that within the environmental context of children, five environmental systems influence their lives. The environmental systems include:

- The microsystem
- The mesosystem
- The exosystem
- The macrosystem
- The chronosystem

These systems of the environmental context intertwine with the process of human development and impact how individuals behave.[1]

To acquire a succinct understanding of these systems, it is important to define several terms: ecology, microsystem, mesosystem, exosystem, macrosystem, and chronosystem. Ecology entails the study of relationships that connect all individuals with society. Microsystem refers to the setting in which an individual lives.[2] Mesosystem involves the relationships of family experiences to school experiences; school experiences to church experiences; and family experiences to peer experiences.

Exosystem comprises social settings such as work, media, school, and local and government agencies. Macrosystem includes the larger cultural context, norms, customs, beliefs, laws, and relationships. Chronosystem refers to patterning of environmental events and transactions during the life course.[3]

Intertwining with children, within their environmental context, there are several ways in which human development unfolds:

- It results from the interaction between the individual and the environment.
- It manifests in a variety of settings, including the physical, the social, the intellectual, the economical, and the political.
- It evolves through advanced relationships within those settings.
- It emerges through interactions within various settings of society.

These emergences of the human developmental process indicate that human development is complex. And if a process focuses solely on matching categories such as income of family, intellectual ability, or ethnicity, pertinent information about an individual's situation may not be unveiled. Bronfenbrenner's model captures how people make sense of their circumstances and how their understanding influences their behavior.[4]

In addition, it recognizes that different people may react differently to the same situation. For example, an individual's history, expectations, and feelings will likely dictate how he or she perceives or responds to a particular situation. The feelings of individuals when confronted with stressful situations, such as contingencies established by federal and state legislators regarding employment opportunities, health care services, welfare benefits, and judicial decrees, will impact their behavior.

In these situations, the response of one person may be positive, while the response of another person may be negative.[5] Individuals tend to demonstrate the behavior embedded within the environment in which they live and develop. And this is one reason why educators cannot fully grasp the behavior of students if they rely solely on observations and clinical measurements. It is essential that they acquire relevant information from social, physical, and cultural environments.[6]

Assessing the environmental context, beginning with family contexts and extending to global contexts, will produce relevant information pertaining to human experiences. The experiences of individuals within the five environmental systems nestle one within the other. For example, when children experience parental rejection, they may have difficulty with adjustment to school, which involves the microsystem, the mesosystem, the macrosystem, the exosystem, and the chronosystem.

Reflecting the microsystem, remember, family is with whom most children live and develop. Relationships involving family experiences to school experiences reflect the mesosystem. School is one of the social settings where customs, beliefs, and laws are practiced to which children are exposed. Practices, customs, and beliefs are what impact the events in schools that children experience.

Involving the microsystem, the mesosystem, the macrosystem, the exosystem, and the chronosystem, engagement with certain peers may cause family turmoil, which affects children. This could impact the family experiences within social settings such as work, media, school, and local and government agencies. Family life is affected by the job experiences of parents, which include travel requirements, job stress, and earnings.

Although children are not involved in their parent's workplace, external events, such as loss of employment, job promotion, or extended work hours of their parents, impact the family life of children. In the larger cultural context, the macrosystem strongly influences roles, norms, customs, beliefs, laws, and relationships. For example, children usually act differently within their own family than in a classroom.

The expectation in the classroom often requires children to sit at a desk during most of the course of the school day and complete their work. In contrast, at home, the expectation to sit at a desk for long hours, working on school assignments, is not imposed on children. In fact, role expectations differ significantly from one setting to another.[7]

The chronosystem, or person-process-content-time, theory refers to patterning of environmental events and transactions during the life course. Examples of environmental events are divorce and remarriage, which often negatively impact children. When divorce and remarriage occur, children are confronted with a different family structure to which to adjust.

They are often faced with a variety of adjustments, such as parental and sibling relations, changing of schools, and meeting and making new friends. Adjustment issues related to aspects of society involve the microsystem, the mesosystem, the exosystem, the macrosystem, and the chronosystem, and they are linked with structure, economics, and values, which highly impact the fate of children.[8] Their development and behavior are linked with environmental systems.

SUMMARY

Educators must recognize that schools do not exist apart from society. The problems of society, such as a struggling economy, creating unemployment of students' parents, affect the lives of children. Other issues, such as poverty, substance abuse, suicide, crime, and teen pregnancy, are what some children routinely attempt to cope with.

When educators work with children, what they see externally provides little information on what is actually happening internally with the children. In their efforts to help children work to their acme of potential, educators must not look solely at factors such as income, ethnicity, or intellectual ability. They must consider other factors that shape child development.

Educators must be willing to acknowledge that how children perceive their circumstances will dictate their actions. The various systems within children's environmental context do influence their development. Often, their experiences, resulting from the microsystem, the macrosystem, the exosystem, and the chronosystem, guide their actions. With this awareness, it should be conceivable that the "Hook" is what will help children succeed.

NOTES

1. A. T. Morales, B. W. Sheafor, *Social work a profession of many faces* (Needham, MA: Allyn and Bacon, 1998).
2. J. Lerner, *Learning disabilities* (Boston: Houghton Mifflin, 2003).
3. Santrock, 61-9.
4. Zanden, 133-86.
5. U. Bronfenbrenner, *The ecology of human development* (Cambridge, MA: Harvard University, 1979).
6. M. P. Nicholas, R. C. Schwartz, *Family therapy: Concepts and methods*, Rev. ed. (Needham Heights, MA: Allyn & Bacon, 2001).
7. D. S. Delcampo, R. L. Delcampo, *Taking sides: Clashing views on controversial issues in childhood and society*, Rev. ed. (Guilford, Connecticut: Dushkin McGraw-Hill, 1998).
8. J. Weinstein, *Social and cultural change*, (Needham Heights, NJ: Allyn & Bacon, 1997).

Chapter Five

Ecological Factors Influencing the Behavior of Children

"Of all properties which belong to honorable men, not one is so highly prized as that of character."
—Henry Clay

The development of children is influenced by numerous factors within their environment. Those factors can have positive influences and they can have negative influences. In either case, children's behavior is a reaction to their environment. Their behavior also reflects their adaptation to their environment. Ideally, a healthy environment for children is what we strive for.

The term *ecological* refers to various environments within which an individual lives and grows.[1] Within the lives of children, three major components have been identified as influencing their behavior: family, peers, and community. For decades, researchers and society alike have considered family as the primary system that actuates the development of children. Factors including family structure and family functionalism have greatly impacted child development.[2]

The term *family* refers to a group of two or more people who are related by blood, marriage, or adoption and typically live together. Family also entails social units, including father, mother, child or children, and other relatives who interact with each other in respective positions. The culture of family imparts customs, values, morals, and beliefs that shape human development.[3]

Through family interactions, the foundation for children is inherited as they acquire varied skills of competency. The success and the productivity of children are linked with love, guidance, and support from family. Through family, when children's developmental needs are met, they are able to thrive.[4]

FAMILY INFLUENCE ON STAGES OF CHILD DEVELOPMENT

At birth, family members are expected to influence the social-emotional development of their children through teaching trust and providing them a sense of security. When this happens, normal attachment is possible. Later, during the stage of early childhood, family is responsible for teaching children social and problem-solving skills, self-help skills, to follow directions, to get along with others, and to share and cooperate. This is the period of development where growth is evident in children's cognitive, social, and physical skills.

During middle childhood, family is expected to guide children in mastering intellectual skills needed to decipher acceptable behavior from unacceptable behavior. Children learn that there are consequences for inappropriate behavior and that their actions can lead to positive or negative outcomes.

To increase acceptable behavior, family must establish clear limits and rules that will help children understand social boundaries and limits. Rules, routines, and responsibilities must be established to eliminate chaos, simplify expectations, and identify individual roles. When children learn responsibilities and initiative, commitment and motivation are possible.

The developmental transition from middle childhood to adolescence is highlighted with negotiation between family and child. Decisions are made that will have phenomenal consequences for children. This is the period when the challenge of autonomy is encountered, causing children to have impaired judgment and confusion of positive role and positive identity.

Adolescents find they are unable to develop the independence that they are striving to obtain. As they encounter puberty, they experience psychological changes, including mood swings, aggression, and depression. These psychological changes of adolescents are what often create havoc for the family.[5]

Other problems that the family encounters with adolescents include teen suicide, depression, and substance abuse. Teen suicide is the third leading cause of death. Depression is the leading, and substance abuse is the second. The likelihood of these issues is decreased when family members closely monitor and supervise their adolescents.[6]

FAMILY STRUCTURE OF AFRICAN AMERICANS

The African-American family has been stereotyped by the term *traditional American family* because within the culture, the term *family* commonly means members beyond father, mother, son, daughter, and other relatives, to include all household members.

Grandparents and informally adopted household members are often considered immediate family. The success and productivity of their children are linked with the involvement of not only the immediate family, but also the extended family. The love, the guidance, and the support of all family members help the children thrive.

Even as far back as 1807 this was seen when slavery caused slave owners to make decisions that directly controlled African Americans' family unity. Parents and children were sold away from each other at the discretion of slave owners, and children's survival was contingent upon the parental role of other adults. This method of dissolving their intact family was considered one of the most pervasive attacks against African Americans.

During slavery, regardless of household composition, African Americans considered all individuals who nurtured and supported their children as family. At that time, the concept of family was pedifocal. The pedifocal conceptualization of family assumes that children belong to the community and are the responsibility of any adult who contributes to their welfare.

African-American families often use the pedifocal concept for informal adoption of their children under conditions of poverty. Using informal adoption, African-American children would receive financial assistance from one source and nurturance and socialization from another source. This type of survival became a strategy with which they developed enormous experience.

Their family structure has been further impacted by countless situations, including, but not limited to: single female–headed households, divorce, unsuitable housing, unemployment, teen pregnancy, and inadequate health care and child care. To help with child care and child rearing, African Americans frequently had to use extended family. Extended family would often provide discipline and supervision.

Following the 1960s, after various movements, African-American families were able to assume active roles in inspiring values, beliefs, and morals in their children. They began to promote positive outcomes of their children, offering support, nurture, and discipline. Their individual needs were not placed ahead of their children.

Studies have adequately documented that when African Americans' intact family was disrupted, the disruption often denied them the opportunity to promote developmental skills of their children during the critical period of child development. This is significant because the future of children is shaped more during their early experiences than during any other periods.

Children's development is promoted when they find their anchor and source of security in their family. The security experienced through family enables children to endure a variety of challenges. Their major challenges are often associated with family structuralism and family functionalism.

FAMILY STRUCTURALISM

Structuralism refers to order or an organized pattern in which family members interact in relationships. The interaction of family members within their culture poses structural constraints that are often disregarded by educators. For instance, within the context of family, structuralism subsumes the overall family organization in which interactions are embedded.

In the vast majority of cases, it is the structure that influences the decisions of individuals. When individuals make changes, their structural context is modified. The purpose of modifying the family structure is to elicit a more competent family system.

Disturbingly, this was not what happened following the 1960s. For many children, their family structure was not a competent family system; instead, demographic trends such as cohabitation, marriage, divorce, and remarriage weakened family stability and decreased family size.

One consequence of the structural changes of family was that it caused many children to live in homes without the support of both biological parents. In fact, it was reported that in 1970, nearly 80 percent of all children in the United States lived with two parents, while in 1996 only 71 percent of all children in the United States lived with both parents.

During the 1980s, when industrialization created shifts in the economy, expanding international competition for products and cheap labor, family structuralism dramatically changed. The industrial restructuring exacerbated family structure changes, generating increases in single-parent families and higher unemployment rates while decreasing employment opportunities. These changes in family structure undermined the functionalism of the "traditional nuclear family," forming other family structures, including stepparent or blended families, extended families, and gay or lesbian families, all of which impact children.

Structure of the Nuclear Family

The traditional nuclear family consists of two biological parents and children. One parent, often the mother, stays at home while the father provides for the family. Within this family structure, children benefit from same-sex and opposite-sex role models.

The environment of this family is generally safe, warm, and nurturing for children. Most mothers of the nuclear family aspire to stay at home with their children. Their focus is to make a happy nest for their children by providing structure to daily living and creating a sense of security.

Following events such as World War II, the atomic bomb, the Holocaust, the women's rights movement, and Watergate, the structure of the nuclear family experienced major changes with dramatic increases in single-parent households. Gaining national attention, the number of married women who worked outside the home with children under the age of six increased from 11 percent in the 1950s to 60 percent in 2000. A positive was that the proportion of children in the United States living with both biological parents increased from 51 percent in 1991 to 56 percent in 1996 and 68 percent in 1999.

The proportion of children in two-parent homes increased from 68 percent in 1999 to 69.1 percent in 2000. It was estimated that the proportion of children who lived with one parent was 25 percent in 1999, and the proportion of children who lived with stepparent or blended family was 8 percent.

Since 1995, the proportion of African-American children living in two-parent homes increased from 34.8 percent to 38.9 percent in 2000. These changes in family resulted in an increase in employment of women with children under age six and a decrease in the number of single-parent families.

Today, in the United States, these types of events continue to impact family structure. And little has changed about the traditional nuclear family structure being widely considered the norm, leaving other family structures perceived as deficient or dysfunctional. This does not mean that there is no recognition that other family structures are healthy and that children do benefit from relationships in other families, including single-parent families.

Structure of the Single-Parent Family

Single parenthood is the result of nonmarital childbearing, divorce, a deceased parent, or single-parent adoption. At all socioeconomic levels, single parenthood exists. In the United States, single-parent families account for 50 percent of all families. And the highest number of single parents is among African-American women.

Data reveal that single parenthood tends to be problematic and a risk factor for normal child development. The main reason for this is children do not have the guidance and supervision of two parents. Another concern of single parenthood is that it mirrors inadequate income, frequent changes in routines, poor-quality child care, and unsafe neighborhoods.

Researchers have found that children of single parents tend to perform at a lower academic rate in school because their resources and social experiences are limited. There is often a disparity between the quantity of resources and the quality of social experiences available to these children than those of two-parent families. Children of single parents tend to repeat grades, score lower on tests, and drop out of school.

When single parents do not strive to balance the demands of work and the responsibilities of parenting, their children's problems tend to escalate. For these reasons, they sometimes have to work flexible schedules and/or accept part-time work, acknowledging that with two parents, their children have a chance for increased parental interventions. To help their children, extended family members often help single parents by providing child care.

Structure of the Extended Family

The extended family is associated with the "sandwich generation" because families are managing their children and their aging parents. The household of extended family consists of members outside the nuclear family unit who are related by blood, marriage, or adoption, sharing domestic and familial obligations. Several social issues, including economics, demographics, and cultural factors, perpetuate extended families.

To combat problems of insufficient and limited resources within family households, the extended family functions as an economic safeguard. When employment is lost, several family members may reside in the same household. In an effort to support and stabilize the intact family, elderly parents often move in with their children and provide child care to their grandchildren.

In addition, elderly parents live with their children to combine their income for management of daily living needs such as housing and health care. Even with this arrangement, some children's basic needs are unmet. They continue be without adequate food and clothing.

Data show that single mothers and minorities are among the highest number of individuals that subsist in the extended family unit. According to the U.S. Census Bureau (2001), 5 percent of all children in the United States lived with grandparents, and 12.3 percent of African-American children lived with grandparents who were the primary caregivers. It is estimated that the proportion of extended family household will increase to a rate of 5 to 10 percent of all households.

Within African-American families, three generations may interact to help provide children a sense of belonging. Their extended family household composition may include the single mother and her pregnant teens. The unmarried teens, with children of their own, are often without financial resources to maintain a home and care for their children independently.

African Americans, more often than European Americans, are more likely to live in extended families because of economic hardships. Their struggles result from inadequate food, money, and/or housing. Similar to other families, many African-American families require regular child-care services from grandparents or other extended kin who reside in the home. Although the pool of generated resources influences the prospect of social mobility and child monitoring and supervision, some children need additional support.

Even in situations where both parents work and some grandparents move in to help with both child care and housework, some children still do not have sufficient funds to purchase lunch at school. The expectations of the family that are expressed to children by their grandparents often do not result in compliance.

Another concern associated with extended family is that extended family members can create dependency or irresponsibility in some single mothers. Responsible actions such as preparing meals and monitoring health needs of their children are assumed by grandparents. Some grandparents attend school conferences and help their grandchildren with school projects.

Other concerns are hierarchy and boundary issues for children. Children will conveniently use hierarchy and boundaries to their advantage. When an extended family household consists of uncle, aunt, and grandmother, children may become confused or receive conflicting information about rules and expectations as they do in blended or stepparent families.

Structure of the Blended or Stepparent Family

Stepfamilies are instant families that result from divorce and remarriage. When this happens, children often develop psychological problems. The primary problem evolves from custody disputes. And the secondary problem emerges from child support.

Mothers typically maintain custody of the children after the marriage is dissolved. The living arrangement of mother and stepfather is the most common form of stepparent or blended family. In 1990, the Vital Statistics Report indicated that 10.3 percent of children in the United States lived with their stepfather and biological mother, 0.6 percent lived with their stepmother and biological father, and 9.8 percent lived with a combined stepfather and stepmother.

In 1997, of all children in America, 50 percent lived in some form of stepfamily relationship. This percentage suggests that the number of stepfamilies will exceed the number of nuclear families in the next decade. This will cause these children to experience adjustment difficulties.

Some children will come to school unwilling to cooperate with their teachers. Some children will come to school and cause problems for other students. And some children will come to school and isolate self.

Other issues children in this family structure experience include conflict and confusion regarding loyalty feelings of love and affection toward their biological parents and attachment to their stepparents. Compounding these feelings, stress and chaos engulf them. They do not welcome the lack of privacy or a bed of their own in which to sleep. They deplore having to adhere to multiple authority figures and sharing their clothes.

The psychosomatic symptoms that they tend to develop include headaches and stomachaches. They complain of health issues, which are used as defense mechanisms and tend to reflect the resentment they have toward their biological parents for abandoning them or not visiting regularly. Unlike children of the nuclear family, these children experience a broader range of adjustment problems. Their problems often include:

- Feelings of insecurity
- Sadness
- Anger
- Helplessness

These feelings of children are what educators commonly see. These feelings of children are what often cause some children to perform poorly in school and/or display aberrant behavior. And these feeling of children are what educators often do not fully understand.

In the stepfamily situation, if both biological parents maintain regular contact with their children, the children are better able to deal with their feelings. After adequate time has passed, possibly a period of two to three years, the behaviors displayed typically subside. Children begin to engage with others.

Among these feelings of children, they are more prevalent in younger children than in adolescents. Adolescents in this family structure tend to identify with their biological mother as the primary disciplinarian, while adolescents of the nuclear family have a tendency to identify with their biological father. This is the key reason why discipline has been considered the highest area of dispute between the biological parent and the stepparent.

Conflicts between the biological parent and the stepparent often cause adolescents to spend less time at home and more time with their friends. The continued unsupervised time with their peers increases the possibility for a variety of negative outcomes. The negative outcomes associated with children in this family structure include:

- Poor academic achievement
- School dropout
- Sexual activity
- Substance abuse
- Delinquency

Another issue for children of stepfamilies is family relocation. When their families move, they often have to change schools and make new friends. While this is true of other family structures, children of stepfamilies may encounter relocation more. In the event of legal matters, stepchildren have no automatic legal rights or commitments, including inheritance benefits that biological children are afforded.

Some positives associated with the stepfamily structure include:

- The development of strategies to resolve conflicts and practices of compromise
- A broader family unit and a larger network of support
- Relationships with their stepsiblings beyond the marriage of their stepparents
- Opportunities for exposure to different expectations, habits, attitudes, values, and rituals
- Extended family members who help foster relationship building
- Extended or stepparent family members who mediate new relationships between parents, stepparents, stepchildren, and stepsiblings when there are family difficulties

The extended or stepparent family also provides child care when the noncustodial parent cancels the plan to take the child for the weekend. This is extremely helpful because supervision and monitoring can be provided. All children, including children of gay and lesbian families, greatly benefit from such.

Structure of the Gay or Lesbian Family

The gay or lesbian family comprises a same-sex union, partnership, or marriage. Prior to the 1960s, this was the family structure that was viewed as preposterous. With much visibility, today, it is considered one of the many normal family structures. In the United States, the gay and lesbian population is at least one million.[7]

Although the recognition of gay and lesbian unions in the late 1980s decreased the polarization, we know some children from these families continue to be stigmatized, teased, and bullied. Proponents argue that society seems to disregard the fact that there is no significant difference between children reared by heterosexual parents than those reared by homosexual parents.

The children of gay and lesbian families are no more likely to have tendencies toward homosexuality than children raised by heterosexual parents. In addition to proponents, studies have found that there is no significant difference between children reared by heterosexual parents and those raised by homosexual parents.

In fact, it was found that there is no major difference of gender identity, self-concept, intelligence, personality characteristics, emotional adjustment, behavioral problems, peer relations, or the likelihood of being sexually abused between children reared by heterosexual parents and those reared by homosexual parents. The difference between children reared by heterosexual parents and those reared by homosexual parents is the stereotypes.

In addition, there has been no evidence to support unhealthy development of children from gay and lesbian families. Children from gay and lesbian families are able to thrive when given proper care. These children should not be perceived differently from other children. Their development, along with other children, is also shaped by family functionalism.

FAMILY FUNCTIONALISM

Within the context of functionalism, family is described as a system or a group with interrelated parts that function as a whole. When family operates as a whole, several aspects of effective communication exist, including listening and sharing and the ability to discuss sensitive issues calmly and peacefully. As family interacts in unity, relationships are established and cultures or practices are developed. If changes occur in one part, there are consequences for the whole.

There is an intense interdependence among family components. That is, family is part of a larger system, which influences the thoughts and actions of other family members, especially children. For example, the cultural symptomatic behavior of a mother in the family is expressive, while the father's role is instrumental.

This long history of cultural and societal expectations has guided how family attempts to adapt to the environment. Adaptation to the environment can be difficult. Within the environment, adaptation is explained as functionalism.

Functionalism refers to limits or boundaries within the environment. Boundaries that are extremely rigid or diluted create a dysfunctional family structure. Functionalism also defines how the organizational structure of society dictates and restricts its customs and beliefs.

Using family as a subsystem of the larger systems, family operates within a set of rules governing those who will be included in the subsystem. Family dictates how those included in the subsystem will interact with those outside the subsystem. To impart functionalism for children, family establishes rules as a major part of discipline.

Discipline: An Influence on Family Functionalism

Discipline encompasses three major components: rules, routines, and responsibilities. With consistent rules, routines, and responsibilities, structure is provided for children that creates a sense of order and predictability. Children benefit tremendously from routines that offer stability, security, organizational skills, direction, and order. More importantly, routines eliminate chaos.

When using rules as a part of discipline, a major advantage of rules is the limitations that are imposed. For example, rules set boundaries to properly guide children. Children learn acceptable behavior when social boundaries and limits are enforced. When rules are established, it is important to consider rules that are reasonable and enforceable.

To correct and guide children's aberrant behavior, screaming, belittling, and ridiculing are inappropriate. Children don't feel good about themselves after being yelled at, hit, or slapped. Instead of belittling, praise is a form of discipline that is as equally effective as correction and guidance. When children have done well, compliment and encourage them. A sincere hug or being told that they are loved affords them encouragement.

Another effective tool for guidance and correction is apprising children of their mistakes. Children benefit from being told what they have done wrong and given clear examples of appropriate behavior. When children have information that is concise, they will make better choices. The relationship between what they do and what happens as a result of their actions is better understood.

LEARNING THEORIES

One of the best approaches used for teaching children acceptable behavior is modeling. Alike, researchers Jean Piaget and Albert Bandura found that learning is acquired through observation. The individual imitates those behaviors observed.

Bandura's theory of social learning and Kohlberg's theory of moral development illustrate that children perceive what is morally right and morally wrong by the actions of others. Similarly, Piaget found that from birth, children are active receivers of environmental stimulation. Their morality is based on the constraints imposed by adults. Children use information accumulated from the environment to construct perspectives of how the world functions and how to interact within it.

In Thorndike's study, he showed that children's learning manifests through direct experiences within the environment. His work revealed that it is not only the culture, but also the home environment that reinforces what children learn. Their varied behavior patterns are reinforced by different cultures.

Another significant example of learning within the environment is Skinner's study of operant conditioning. He found that behavior is controlled through environmental forces such as rewards and punishment. When environmental forces are punitive or when there are consequences, behavior changes. In order to change children's behavior, we must understand their perception of their environment. This includes their feelings, attitudes, and abilities that operate within their perceptions.

Within the environment, there is a connection between people and the cultural context in which they interact. For example, Skinner's illustration of operant conditioning validated that an individual is what he or she has been reinforced to be through consistent observation of behavior patterns.

PEER GROUPS

Reinforcement through observation emerges from others, especially peers. Peers have been credited as the secondary source of influence on child development. They influence the social development of children toward acceptable and unacceptable behaviors and values. Beginning at an early age and increasing in frequency, children are immersed in countless relationships with other children.

At age two, they spend approximately 10 percent of their time engaging in activities with peers. At age 11, they spend more than 50 percent of their time with peers. During the period of adolescence, their time spent with adults generally diminishes.[8]

From each other, peers learn during their social encounters. Their exposure to and their interaction with others promote social competency. They gain skills in dealing with conflict and managing emotions. They obtain immediate feedback that helps them critically assess their behavior.

Without peers, children are less likely to acquire essential social skills. In fact, studies reveal that there are negative consequences for children who are unable to engage in positive interactions with peers. Those negative outcomes are more prevalent during adolescence.

It is during the period of adolescence when children encounter the challenge of autonomy. Confusion of positive identity and positive role often lead to impaired judgment. Peers take precedence over family. Unintentionally, peers assume some of the parental roles of support and guidance because some children value their peer relationships over those with their parents.

Rather than with their parents, many children experience their greatest frustrations and happiest moments with their peers. They use peers to serve as a yardstick of comparison regarding physical and psychological growth. They secure feedback about their abilities and ideas from each other. Their affiliation with positive peers establishes a safeguard against negative influences.

Among African-American males, there is an attempt to conceal their desire to engage in meaningful relationships. Instead of displaying their true feelings of hopelessness and despair, they will present a facade of "cool posing" to camouflage those feelings. Their intended image to be cool is then misread and viewed as aggressive and violent behavior.

To fulfill their need for acceptance, they look to their peers regarding styles and trends of clothing and music.[9] Those positive interactions with their peers build social relationships. If they have concerns about sex and drugs, they will often express them with peers rather than adults. They tend to share their secrets with peers instead of adults.

From their peers, they gain a substantial source of security. And when they are accepted by their peers, they tend to be mentally healthy. On the other hand, when they experience rejection and isolation, their social developmental skills are hampered.

Rejected Peers

Unlike children who are accepted by their peers, rejected children are characterized as low social status. The factors that contribute to children's low social status include:

- Appearance
- Intelligence
- Athletic ability
- Name
- Disabilities

Once social status is determined, children receive consideration from peers based on that status. With the use of sociometric ratings and nomination measures, a study of peer relationships of rejected children revealed several significant concerns:

- Peers do not consider rejected children as their friends.
- Peers do not want a relationship with rejected children.
- Peers have negative attitudes toward rejected children.
- New behaviors of rejected children do not result in peer acceptance.

This suggests that even when rejected children employ appropriate social skills, they continue to experience negative peer response. They have greater difficulty engaging in ongoing activities because social networks and groups are formed with peers of similar social status. This explains why low-status children have only low-status children with whom to interact. If their social networking and grouping comprise only low-status peers, then the quality of their social interactions and opportunities to participate in positive and cooperative interactions will not be as high as those of affluent students.

Peer Relations

In addition to the negative influences of peers, there are positive influences. These peer groups discourage antisocial behavior and school failure that are exacerbated by maladaptive interactions and learned patterns of inappropriate behavior within peer relationships. With positive peer influence, normal social and emotional development increases. The advantages of positive peer groups include:

- Decreases in school failure
- Reduction in delinquency
- Less school violence
- Reduced substance abuse

On the other hand, it is the affiliation with antisocial peers that often leads to problems such as substance abuse and school failure. Other factors that influence the quality of children's social systems include:

- Aggression
- Poor impulse control behavior
- Bullying
- Teen pregnancy

Children who associate with peers who drink and smoke tend to do so themselves. When children select peers, they are choosing who will influence them and whom they will influence. The children who drop out of school are more likely to experience higher levels of unemployment and receive lower wages than high-school graduates.

Dropouts, more than graduates, tend to be recipients of welfare and engage in illegal activities. This means that it is important to encourage quality peer socialization because it is the peers who resist aberrant behavior who will likely discourage it. In contrast, it is those peers who engage in antisocial behaviors who will likely encourage negative behavior.[10]

COMMUNITY INFLUENCE

The negative behavior and outcomes of children have caused community involvement. Community, for many years, has assumed a vital role in helping to alleviate some of the problems children face. It continues to serve as children's secondary field of interaction. Although there is no common distinguishing quality, community is defined as:

- A subsystem of society
- A macrosystem
- A vital linkage to family

Community's main objective has been to identify the social needs of children and families and develop strategies to meet those needs. The way community has done this is through cooperation, collaboration, and coordination. Its focus continues to be health, welfare, recreation, and child care.

Historical Development of Community

The early historical development of community began in 1870. At that time, community groups organized and evaluated resources that would improve the social conditions of impoverished individuals. The most visible groups were community chest and charity organizations.

Since that time, community has operated, maintaining significant roles in the lives of children by:

- Providing them with varied positive adult exposure, such as mentors, tutors, youth facilitators, and coaches
- Enriching their horizon
- Expanding their experiences
- Advancing their opportunities
- Nurturing their interactions

For many children, community has even served as extended family. Their relentless work is what has sustained and advanced the level of services available to children.

Community Support

Children's motivation and adjustment have been shaped by community efforts which have enabled them to:

- Experience a sense of coherence
- Manage school hassles
- Attend school daily
- Comply with school rules
- Make academic improvements

Community intervention also has formed partnerships that provide children access to resources, training, and opportunities that have supported their intellectual growth and productivity. An example of a community-school partnership is Highland Park School in Michigan, where the involvement led to positive student behavior. After one school year, the referrals for student disruptive behavior decreased by 75 percent.

In another community partnership that focused on children's social support networks, students' delinquent behavior was deterred. Their involvement showed an increase in school readiness of children. These forms of accomplishments highlight the vital role partnerships play in improving the outcomes of children.

External and Internal Assets of the Community

In communities, four major external assets and four major internal assets exist. The external assets include:

- Support
- Empowerment
- Boundaries
- Expectations and constructive use of time

Support consists of family, school, and other adults. Empowerment refers to community engaging children in activities of value that promote a sense of worth. Children are viewed as resources and having power over their lives. Boundaries and expectations refer to the guidelines and standards that family, school, and other adults establish.

High expectations, adult role models, and positive peer influences are encouraged to help children. Constructive use of time includes creative and religious activities, youth programs, and quality family experiences. With these external assets, a difference is made in the lives of children.

The internal assets include:

- Commitment to learning
- Positive values
- Social competencies
- Positive identity

These internal assets encourage achievement and character development. With commitment to learning, there is support of partnerships with schools to increase student achievement and motivation.

Positive values advocate caring, integrity, honesty, and responsibility. Social competencies facilitate the development of decision-making and conflict resolution skills. Positive identity promotes self-esteem and a sense of worth.

Partnerships with governmental agencies such as mental health and social service departments function in part to meet the social-emotional needs of needy children and their families. Some past community and federal programs, including Manpower Development and Training, Comprehensive Employment Training Act, Job Training and Partnership Act, Head Start, and Family Assistance, have provided educational and job training assistance.

Their primary aim has been to stimulate the economic levels of the needy families and their children. Through these programs, children who have experienced transitions, changes, and challenges have greatly benefited because of the involvement community has shown.[11]

The Historical Role of the Church

Being an essential part of a community, the church has operated to transcend values, morals, and beliefs. From the beginning of recorded history, the Christian Church has taught faith and that a better life is possible. It has historically shown concern for the needs of individuals, particularly the poor and the oppressed. Its overall focus has been love, charity, and righteousness.

Within the Christian Church, a wide variety of denominations, sects, and cults exist, supporting the Christian mission of giving. Christian churches collected funds as early as 1536 to help the poor, the oppressed, the lame, and the sick. Within Christian churches, provisions were established to protect children and prevent incidences of child neglect and abuse.

The Christian Church gave precedence to emergency situations of families and children. The needs and protection of the sick, widows, and orphans were considered important. The Christian Church served, in many instances, as a charity institution, providing food, shelter, and clothing to the needy. However, in situations of immoral behaviors such as drinking and gambling, the Christian Church denied assistance to individuals.

Children needing temporary housing were provided shelter by the Christian Church in facilities such as Lutheran Homes for Children, Episcopal Homes for Children, the Baptist Homes for Children, summer camps, and Protestant social agencies. These church-affiliated facilities supported religious values and norms. The rule of fair play, such as "Do unto others as you would have them do unto you," was encouraged.

For centuries, among generations of families, including African Americans, the church taught conformity. In African American churches, children were taught how to get along with others and the spiritual dimensions of humanity in efforts to guide their understanding of a "higher being." As they acquired a greater understanding of a "higher being," the expectation was that they show discipline and social control.

The expectation of adolescents who attended church regularly and heard messages that encouraged abstaining from sex was to refrain from premarital sex. On the other hand, the adolescents who attended church irregularly often demonstrated a more permissive attitude toward premarital sex than those who frequently heard abstaining messages.

The spirituality of the Christian Church of African Americans encouraged and supported a personal relationship with God. These teachings continue to be found in many African-American churches today, as they are in other churches.

In daily conversations, African Americans often speak of God as a positive influence in their lives. Even during periods of life-threatening situations such as war and disaster, their awareness of a "higher being" generates hope for a brighter tomorrow. Their belief in a "higher being" seems to be a factor in their resilience.

African Americans often use the church as a vehicle for releasing their emotional tension and stress. In school, when this is displayed by African-American children, it is not recognized as stress; instead, their emotional outburst is often perceived as disruptive behavior.

SUMMARY

The environment of children greatly impacts their behavior. They are influenced by every aspect of their environment. They imitate what they see and hear. And they react to what they see and hear.

All children are not from the traditional nuclear family structure that provides them with two parents. Their family structure may comprise both parents, a mother only, a father only, grandparents, stepparents, and gay or lesbian parents. Family structuralism will dictate the resources that are available to children. Family functionalism will impact how children behave.

In addition, who children befriend will affect their behavior. Their peers can have a positive influence as well as a negative influence. Both supervision and monitoring can decrease negative behavior. When limits and boundaries are established, the functioning of children improves.

A barrier for some children is that their environmental settings have not afforded them the developmental stimulation needed to adequately thrive. Normal child development did not occur for one reason or another. Support systems such as peers and community were not sought or available. Most importantly, their family structure negatively influenced their family functioning.

NOTES

1. Lerner, 112-13.
2. *Encyclopaedia Britannica.* "Family". http://www.britannica.com/eb/article?eu=118049& tocid=0 April, 12, 2002.
M. N. Collison, "For Dr. Mincy, saving fragile families is personal," *Black Issues in Higher Education*, 16 no.5, (1999): 277-80.
4. W. H. Chafe, R. Gavins, R.Korstad, *Remembering Jim Crow: African Americans tell about life in the segregated south*, (New York: The New Press, 2001).

5. R. L. Jarrett, L. M. Burton, "Dynamic dimensions of family structure in low-income African American families: Emergent themes in qualitative research," *Journal of Comparative Family Studies* 30 no. 2, (Spring 1999): 177-93.
6. D. Blankenborn, "The reappearing nuclear family," *First Things: A Monthly Journal of Religion and Public Life*, (2002, January): 20-26.
7. S. L. Rosenberg, L. M. McKeen, "Positive Peer Groups reclaim rejected kids," *Education Digest* 65 no. 4 (December 1999): 22-28.
8. M. Duncan, R. Cohen, "Liking within the peer group as a function of children's sociometric status and sex," *Child Study Journal* 25 no. 4, (1995): 265-88.
9. P. Stevens, J. Griffin, "Youth high-risk behaviors: Survey and results," *Journal of Addiction and Offender Counseling* 22 no. 1, October, 2001): 31-48.
10. D. Davies, "Powerful partnerships among schools, parents, and communities," *Education Digest* 66 no.2, (October 2000): 41-45.
11. L. Kowaleski-Jones, "Staying out of trouble: Community resources and problem behavior among high-risk adolescents," *Journal of Marriage and Family* 62 no. 2, (May 2000): 449-65.

Part II

Strategies for Closing the Achievement Gap

INTRODUCTION

"There is a destiny that makes us brothers: / None goes his way alone: / All that we send into the lives of others / Comes back into our own."
—Edwin Markham

Chapter 3 documented the impact of the environment on human development. There was widespread agreement among theorists that a healthy environment promotes healthy development. Studies revealed that the development of children is influenced in a variety of ways and settings. Family was recognized as being most significant and having the most influence on the lives of children.

For educators, this means parents would be some of the people with whom you would seek to partner in order to improve student performance. Even if it appears that parents are disinterested, it would still be wise to seek their involvement. It may be determined that the parents who seem detached are the parents who are experiencing some form of crisis.

As the secondary source of influence on children, peers have the ability to influence positive behavior as well as negative behavior. The goal must be to link peers with positive peers in order to increase the likelihood of positive behaviors. Educators and parents must never discount the aggrandized asset of peers in the lives of children.

Other environmental systems such as community and school also influence child development. In the community, children are exposed to and engaged in various programs and activities. Without those programs and activities, some children would not have some of the same positive experiences and opportunities that other children have.

Activities such as plays, reading enrichment summer programs, scholarships, and field trips are often sponsored by the community, offering accessibility for many children. The involvement in these types of programs richly enhances children's development. Exposure to extracurricular activities is what many parents desire but often cannot afford for their children.

The environmental systems have individual yet intertwining influence. Systems link the home and the school and the school and the workplace. Society communicates the roles and expectations of the environmental systems.

One expectation is that there will be some form of communication between the home and the school. And if parents want time off from their jobs to attend school conferences, they must communicate with their employer. They must also communicate with their employer if they hope to maintain their jobs.

When the relations between the home and the parent's workplace are not managed properly, problems develop for children. Those problems of the home environment tend to affect children at school. Some children may come to school tardy or without breakfast because their parents work a late-night shift.

These patterns of society, including cultural context, belief systems, customs, roles, relationships, lifestyles, and laws, influence children's development and behavior. In addition, these patterns have a tendency to dictate family functioning. When families are faced with economic hardships caused by societal decisions, resulting in job losses, the lives of children are affected negatively. Their behaviors at school will often reflect problems at home over which they have no control.

Educators, as you consider this, will you respond differently to the children in your school? Do you believe the task of closing the achievement gap is as difficult as perceived? If so, imagine using what helps children perform to their highest level of potential. Then make greater attempts to meet their needs.

The way you can accomplish this is to capture the attention of your students. Similar to what a writer does, use a hook to gain your students' attention. Then apply the "Hook," which simply is love, power, fun, and freedom.

Data supports that children's desire to thrive academically soars when their essential needs are met. One central way that those needs can be met at school is through the actions of educators, especially teachers. Teachers must create an environment of:

- Love
- Power
- Fun
- Freedom

All children, although they have not had the exact same experiences and the exact same opportunities, will benefit from an environment of these four elements.

Chapter Six

Children's Responses to Their School Experience

"The whole art of teaching is only the art of awakening the natural curiosity of young minds for the purpose of satisfying it afterwards; and curiosity itself can be vivid and wholesome only in proportion as the mind is contented and happy."
—Anatole France

When children enter school they encounter difficulties that are often different from what they experience at home. Some of their problems evolve from interactions with students. Other concerns emerge from their teachers or other educators.

TEACHER PERCEPTIONS OF LOW-INCOME STUDENTS

A study revealed the following perceptions some middle-class teachers held regarding low-income students:

- Low-income students are lazy, rebellious, and loving.
- Children from lower socioeconomic status families are more problematic than children from affluent families.
- Low-income students are happy, energetic, and ambitious.[1]

Instead of these perceptions, studies suggest that students greatly benefit from teachers who have experience in working with children from different backgrounds, which would provide a broader understanding of students' needs.[2] To blame poor children for their oppression is unfair.[3]

In a similar study, educators considered African-American children to be low performers. They held this perception even when African American students' academic outcome was positive. The school personnel maintained that the low-income status of children meant low academic performance. This perception of educators was documented as a partial reason why negative stereotypes and inferior educational opportunities exist toward African-American children. The misguided thoughts of educators have caused them to unintentionally neglect to challenge African-American children, thereby encouraging poor academic performance.[4]

Oblivious to the fact that when warmth is meshed with challenging tasks, the performance will likely improve, some teachers accept poor academic performance of some children rather than provide a warm and caring environment. Their reduced expectations in achievement and performance of some African-American children have caused some to expend less effort to achieve when more effort could have led to success.[5]

Among some African-American males, this was found. Instead of exerting more effort to achieve in school, they became disinterested and eventually dropped out of school. Their decision to quit school was reported as possibly one reason why their dropout rate is ten times higher than that of European-American children.[6]

This is one reason why teachers must provide encouragement to students. It is likely that the encouragement will generate students' school interest and improve their school attendance. Interest in school and regular attendance will result in improved performance.

To decrease school dropout rates, higher teacher enthusiasm and student energy are suggested. Several studies found that appreciably, outcomes including attendance rates, dropout rates, and achievement levels were positively influenced by both teacher enthusiasm and student energy.[7] As teachers showed interest in their students and their work, students displayed motivation.

THE VOICES OF STUDENTS

At all levels, including elementary, middle, and high school, some students frequently made or reported the following comments of their teachers:

> You got a "D" because you are a "D" student. I do not like you. You are stupid. You are never going to graduate. Just put your head down on the desk, you are not going to pass the test anyway. My teacher rolls her eyes at me. She yells at me. She talks disrespectful to me. She never smiles at me. My teacher ignores me when I raise my hand to answer the one question of which I have

the correct answer. My teacher embarrasses me in front of my friends. My teacher never explains or discusses homework assignments in class. She gives little to no input regarding assignments.

Following are a few responses of some high-school graduates from my book Shifting the Paradigm: Through the Lens of the Disadvantaged:

> When I recall my school experiences, I cannot think of a teacher or school personnel who said an encouraging word to me. Few teachers were good and many not so good. Some teachers pushed you down so low that you did not know how to get back up. Through the words of their mouth, teachers can help and hinder. My teacher said, "I don't have time to sit and baby you or to take a special interest in your needs." Some teachers "taunted" me, telling me that I would never be "nothing." Instead of helping me, those comments decreased my motivation. One teacher told me if I got my head "screwed on," I could be productive.

Even in a recent survey of 500 dropouts, ages sixteen to twenty-five, their responses were similar to those of other students:

- 47 percent said their classes were not interesting.
- 43 percent said they missed too many days to catch up.
- 45 percent said they entered high school ill prepared from earlier grades.
- 69 percent said they were not motivated to work hard.
- 35 percent said they were failing.
- 32 percent said they left school to get a job.
- 25 percent said they left school to become parents.
- 22 percent said they left school to take care of a family member.

These responses suggest that students are not receiving what they need academically to become productive and successful.

CHILDREN'S VISION FOR THEIR DEVELOPMENT

It is not only the children who come from undesirable homes or dysfunctional families who want acceptance. All children want and desire to be accepted. Universally, all children want:

- Genuine warmth, care, and encouragement
- Acceptance, support, and to be happy
- To be understood and free to be themselves

They want this from not only their family, but also their peers and school personnel, especially their teachers. What reflects in children's actions is the quality of their experiences. When they experience hostility, they will exhibit hostility. When you smile at them, they will smile back at you.

They display inappropriate behavior because they are resentful of others' actions. They suffer in silence without teachers' knowledge. Their behavior varies because every child is unique.

DEJECTED RESPONSES

Again, at every level, including elementary, middle, and high school, children have consistently verbalized:

> My teacher does not like me. She never makes eye contact with me. She gets in my space. She talks disrespectful to me. She tells me that I am dumb. She always frowns at me. She ignores me.

ENVIRONMENTAL EDUCATION

From studies of environmental education in schools, student achievement increases when the environment is improved. The learners' perceptions of the educational environment are important and must be understood. The culture of students must be in the consciousness of educators because students do not regard school in the same way as educators do. Students perceive school in how it affects them. This is one reason why some African-American males' silent response is to expend less effort to achieve success. Their perception of their environment is reduced teacher expectations.

THEIR REALITY

Educators must be persistent in encouraging all children. They must remember that the children who face atrocities and hardships at home are often those who encounter negative experiences at school. Educators must acknowledge that despite the struggles of many children, some come to school to escape a home life of disappointments. Those same children may come to school in search of a healthy meal or any meal at all.

SUMMARY

So as educators consider the unmet needs of students, should they blame them when they do not perform to their potential? Would it serve students best to seek ways to connect with them and offer support to help them excel? Would it require too much to create an environment conducive to learning for these children?

Educators must not forget that from one stage of development to the next, adequate stimulation has not occurred for all children. Their environmental systems have not afforded them normal child development. Some children have and do live in unstable family structures, which have caused, in some instances, divorce, remarriage, and cohabitation. Their family structures vary from nuclear, single-parent, extended family, stepparent, or blended family, to gay and lesbian family and in some instances, placement in foster homes.

Educators must remember that the structuralism of children greatly impacts how the family functions. When structure changes in families, it is difficult to maintain the same rules in the home. If grandparents move in, they have a tendency to give grandchildren privileges that parents may not offer. The routines in families change when their structure changes.

When parents leave supervision to other household members, their children may stay out late with friends or stay up late watching television. This does adversely impact family functionalism. As the family experiences functioning problems, the probability increases for children having functioning problems at school.

As children attempt to form relationships outside their family, they tend to form them with children of similar background. This happens because these children find it difficult to interact with children who do not understand them. It is easier for them to identify with peers who share something in common rather than those who have no clue of what it is like to have major family difficulties.

Even in the community, these same children will often seek relationships with children in organizations with similar backgrounds. These same children are often referred to agencies such as the department of social services and department of juvenile justice to receive services. These community agencies provide support in shaping the development of these children. They strive to link and expose these children to constructive activities sponsored by various community programs.

The community recognizes that the possibility for positive experiences increases when the concept "it takes a village to raise a child" is embraced. The community partners with the school in efforts to help promote children's development and encourage meaningful involvement in the community. It recognizes that children's intellectual development increases when they have positive school experiences as well as a network of support systems.

As educators, you must recognize the value of support networks for children. Sufficient learning will not occur unless children's developmental needs are met. Those needs must be met on a daily basis. To help children feel comfortable and secure at school, all educators, including administrators, must make a conscious effort to produce an environment that is warm and friendly.

Children must feel this from all school personnel they encounter. Their parents must do their part in developing a nurturing environment at home. These actions, which embrace the "Hook," will result in closing the achievement gap.

NOTES

1. J.Q. Wilson, *The marriage problem: How our culture has weakened families*, (New York: Harper Collins, 2002).
2. Palmer et al., 554-65.
3. Morales, 101-31.
4. Anderson, 151-83.
5. E. Kirby, *Shifting the paradigm: Through the lens of the disadvantaged*, (Germany, Lambert Academic Publishing Co. 2009).
6. B. Pytel, "Why do students leave high school without a diploma?" *Educational Issues Suite 101* (2006) retrieved May 15, 2011 from http://www.suite101.com/content/dropout_give-reasons-a8681.
7. T. Loughland, A. T. Reid, A. Petocz, "Young people's conception of environment: A phenomenographic analysis," *Environmental Education Research*, 8 no. 2, (2002): 187-98.

Chapter Seven

Love

"Take love away from life and you take away its pleasures."
—Moliere

There is an overwhelming assumption that teachers decide to teach because they want to be one of the people who make a positive difference in the lives of children they encounter. In order for this to happen, teachers must first employ love. In the classroom, children need to see teachers' sincere sensitivity to their social, emotional, and intellectual needs. Cognition cannot be separated from emotion because there is a correlation between processing and feeling.

In chapter 3 it was reported that human development is influenced by the environment in which children live. Three fundamental domains, including physical, cognitive, and social, affect the environment. These domains are embedded in students' curriculum.

Physically, at school, students utilize their motor skills to complete various tasks. Cognitively, students engage in activities that allow them to problem-solve, interpret, and organize information. Socially, students interact with individuals within the school. Their social skills are significantly enhanced when they form relationships with others.

The connection students experience at school evolves through interacting with others within the environment. Positive actions toward students tend to produce positive responses. Students experience a sense of warmth in the classroom when they believe their teachers care. They develop a sense of trust and a level of physical comfort when they learn that their teachers can be trusted. When teachers attempt to meet their basic needs, a bond is formed.[1]

Instead of a strong emotional attachment, love, in this book, in the school setting simply refers to care. Love is a human essential need that every child aspires to experience, especially at school. Students want their teachers to demonstrate care.

TRY A LITTLE GENTLENESS

Care is typically shown through teachers' constructive mannerisms, which may include, but is not limited to, smiles, warm greetings, politeness, and praises. Students want to experience genuine warmth from their teachers. When students return after being absent several days, instead of overtly, before the class, ridiculing or embarrassing them, covertly, one on one, welcome them back and offer your support to guide them in completing their missed work. This will increase their interest in attending school daily.

Socially, students need to belong and know that they can confide in their teachers. They need to feel acceptance as well as self-worth. Their attitude about school changes when they feel connected. Support, positive regard, and high expectations make it possible for learning to come naturally.

In addition, students want teachers to listen to them; remain nonjudgmental; give them a second chance; and talk to them rather than shout at them. Students want teachers to validate their positive actions. Validation through smiles and kind words lets students know that their teacher cares. When teachers demonstrate acceptance and care, they provide a comfortable environment in which students can learn.

Legendary UCLA basketball coach John Wooden's favorite maxim was, "There is nothing stronger than gentleness." Children are armed with a sense that enables them to learn how to relate to others when a warm and friendly environment is provided. This environment helps children gain social skills that will provide them a strong foundation. After they experience a sense of physical comfort, cognition will emerge.[2]

DEVELOPING THE SCHOOL CLIMATE

Whether at home or at school, children want to feel that they are cared about. They experience care when genuine interest is shown them. A simple way to demonstrate interest is to get to know the student.

Within the school, care must be transmitted directly from the actions of the leadership, meaning the administrator or principal. The administrator must exemplify care in his or her actions toward his or her work, his or her staff, his or her students, and the students' parents. If the administrator does not like his or her work, it will reflect in his or her actions.

At open house, at the beginning of the school year, is an optimum time for administrators to state and demonstrate their commitment to the needs of students and their parents. An example as to how this may be done follows. The administrator states:

> At this school every student is valued. My staff and I appreciate and support diversity and learning differences. This school has a team of dedicated teachers and student support personnel whom I will introduce. [It is important for students as well as their parents to know the staff of the school.] The responsibility of every teacher is to first create an environment that is conducive to learning. These teachers will be instrumental in helping your child perform to his or her fullest potential. At this school, we are a family. And as a family, we work together for the physical, social, emotional, and intellectual growth of every student. To help promote school family unity within this school, and address the physical, social, emotional, and intellectual needs of your child, the student support personnel, including our school counselors, school social worker, school psychologist, and school nurse, may contact you, the expert, regarding your child. The goal of the student support personnel is to provide whatever support possible to help your child achieve academically. [It is important for parents to know that the role of the school social worker is to help the family, not to break up the family. The school social worker is not a department of social services employee.] In the classroom, each teacher will provide a Getting Acquainted form, which will provide information about the teacher and request similar information about the student.

GETTING ACQUAINTED FORM: (TEACHER SAMPLE FORM)

Teacher name: <u>Mary Doe</u>
School address: <u>3113 Trail Lane Pelham, GA</u>
School number: <u>(336) 699-2434</u>
Email address: doe_12@globalnet.com
University last attended: <u>University of Central Michigan</u>
Number of years teaching: <u>5</u>
In my household, I have <u>0</u> children.
I have <u>3</u> brother/s and <u>3</u> sister/s.
For fun I like to <u>dance</u>. I like to <u>go to the movies</u> with my family.
The way I learn best is <u>discussion</u>. What I do well is <u>sing</u>.
The person having the most influence on my life is <u>my mother</u>.
My favorite food is <u>salmon</u>.

My best friend is <u>Neat</u>.
My favorite artist is <u>Kenny G</u>.
My favorite athlete is <u>Michael Jordan</u>.
The person I admire most (my hero) is <u>Barack Obama</u>.
My favorite place to vacation is <u>New York</u>.
My favorite holiday is <u>Thanksgiving</u>.
Something significant I want you to know about me is <u>that
I want all children to be successful. If you need help, please ask me</u>.

GETTING ACQUAINTED FORM: (STUDENT SAMPLE FORM)

Name: <u>Jane Doe</u>
Father's name: <u>John Doe</u>
Mother's name: <u>Mary Hall</u>
Telephone number: <u>(919) 461-2199</u>
Email address: <u>None</u>
Father's place of employment: <u>Hertz Packaging</u>
Mother's place of employment: <u>Pine Haven Nursing Home</u>
In my household, I have <u>2</u> brothers and <u>3</u> sisters.
My <u>grandmother</u> and <u>cousin</u> also live with me.
I have lived at this address <u>2</u> years.
For fun I like to <u>go fishing</u>. I like to <u>eat</u> with my family.
The way I learn best is <u>review schoolwork</u>. What I do well is <u>write</u>.
The person having the most influence on my life is <u>my big brother</u>.
My best friend is <u>Eddie</u>. My favorite food is <u>pizza</u>.
My favorite artist is <u>Justin Timberlake</u>. My favorite athlete is <u>Kobe Bryant</u>.
The person I admire most (my hero) is <u>my father</u>.
My favorite place to vacation is <u>Disney World</u>.
My favorite holiday is <u>Christmas</u>.
Something significant I want you to know about me is that
<u>I am shy; I get embarrassed easily</u>.

BENEFITS OF THE GETTING ACQUAINTED FORM

For teachers, the Getting Acquainted form provides:

- Some essential information about students' household composition.
- A way to identify who is important in the student's life, which will likely be one of the people having some influence on the student.

- Assistance in identifying the learning style of the student.
- A useful tool to understand students' lives, behaviors, and actions. For example, if a student has five or more siblings, he or she may not have a quiet place to study or his or her own bed in which to sleep, which means that the teacher may need to allow time at school for the student to do homework or shorten homework assignments.
- An excellent tool for getting to know students' various family structures. Awareness of family structure is significant because it has been documented that other family structures are also healthy, yet, in the United States, it is the children of other family structures that are often perceived as deficient or dysfunctional while widely accepting the traditional nuclear family as the norm.
- A great source for obtaining information about students' preferences and some of their experiences. The teacher might notice that a student has an affinity for rebuilding cars. That same student may seem disengaged in the classroom. One way to engage that student in a classroom discussion is to design a lesson plan using the curriculum but to add as a theme "Rebuilding a 1957 Chevy." The teacher may never mention the student's name, but after some discussion solicit the student's input.
- Information about students' personality.
- An awareness that a method or style of delivery must be constructed that incorporates information that enables every student to succeed. For example, to get the students engaged, the teacher may use a journey in the mountains, a trip to the beach, making pizza, and so on. With the use of various types of activities to which students can relate, they will be able to use their cognitive skills to assimilate and accommodate. When students are able to relate life experiences with school assignments, they gain a greater understanding. The idea is to encourage student interest and introduce creativity and imagination in problem solving, especially when attempting a task that may seem somewhat difficult.
- An increased awareness of students' environment so that positive responses rather than stereotypical actions will be shown. Students resent teachers responding to them in a negative manner. When an unhealthy environment is created, it greatly interferes with students' ability to perform at their level of academic potential. The goal is to connect with students so that they will connect with you.

Using the Getting Acquainted form, when placing students in groups, teachers will be able to connect students with other students who have similar interests, which will enable them to build relationships. This will help all children experience some form of engagement. And more than any other benefit, the Getting Acquainted form shows students that teachers care about them because the teacher is taking time to get acquainted.

OTHER BENEFITS OF THE GETTING ACQUAINTED FORM

Similar to the benefits for teachers, the Getting Acquainted form provides benefits for administrators and parents. The administrator can use the student Getting Acquainted form to learn about the students in his or her school. The parent can use the teacher Getting Acquainted form to learn about the teachers' experiences and credentials.

The parent may gain some awareness as to why his or her child's teacher responses are what they are, especially if the teacher does or does not have a child or children. The parent action in this case may involve sharing some specific information with the teacher that will help improve his or her child's performance. When parents do this, teachers are better informed, which places them in a position to be more helpful.

The suggested procedure for completing and disseminating the Getting Acquainted form is:

- Student and/or teacher complete form only once.
- Use home base to complete the form.
- Make copies and disseminate to students' other teachers.
- Give each middle- and high-school student a copy of the teacher's Getting Acquainted form so that they can read and share the information on the form with their parents.
- Give parents of the elementary students the Getting Acquainted form for completion and a copy of the teachers' completed forms.

PARENTAL RESPONSIBILITY

In order to better serve students, teachers must not ignore the crucial role that parents play. They must acknowledge that children need their parents to be responsible and that it is important for parents to hear from teachers regarding school expectations. Despite barriers, parents must assume their responsibility of monitoring, observing, and advocating for their children.[3]

Monitoring, awareness, and advocacy increase the likelihood of normal child development. Clearly, beyond parents, there generally is no other source privy to types of information regarding the progress of their child's development. Parents, more than any other source, will have a greater awareness of the physical, cognitive, and social-emotional needs of their children.

The expectation is that parents will meet the physical, cognitive, and social-emotional needs of their children through creating a home environment that is supportive. It is also expected that parents will be the individuals responsible for providing a stable home environment for their children. In doing so, they will provide a home environment that is warm, safe, and friendly, which will enable their children to learn.

They will assume responsibilities of making certain that their children get plenty of sleep each night and consume a nutritious breakfast each morning. Furthermore, parents are expected to provide appropriate clothes for their children. As they assume these responsibilities, the likelihood increases for their children's success.

When parents provide structure in the home, children will be less likely to experience difficulty adjusting to school regimentation. On the other hand, when there is turmoil in the home, children will be more likely to experience difficulty focusing and learning. Difficulties in the home often produce anxiety and depression. Anxiety and depression affect children in several ways:

1. Anxiety and depression adversely affect children's capacity to concentrate or memorize. The emotional energy of children is expended in dealing with inner preoccupations.
2. Anxiety and depression cause children to have low self-esteem. When children experience low self-esteem, they tend to have difficulty handling responsibilities and adapting to unfamiliar situations.
3. Anxiety is highly correlated with learning ability. Children living in chaos tend to perform poorly on IQ tests. Therefore, a supportive home life is crucial to reduce stress in children and to help improve their IQ.

In the midst of a home environment torn by internal discord, the behaviors of children often include:

- Displays of sadness and aggression
- Extreme withdrawal
- Daydreaming
- Headaches and stomachaches
- Failing grades
- Short attention span
- Return to bed-wetting
- Excessive crying and whining

These and other behaviors that students exhibit interfere with their performance, which contributes to academic failure.[4] To address this concern, it is suggested that administrators use open house, at the beginning of the school year, when there are many parents in the school, to recruit ten parents per grade level, preferably males (if not available, use females), to serve as volunteers in the school. Ten parents would be for middle school. For elementary, five parents or fewer per grade level would likely be adequate.

In high schools, parents do not have to be as visible. Their involvement entails monitoring their child's progress frequently and tracking their child's graduation and college requirement needs. High-school parents may join their child's school PTA and possibly one of the school's improvement teams.

At the middle-school level, recruit male volunteers because often boys and girls alike need a male role model. Fathers, grandfathers, boyfriends, uncles, cousins, male church members, and males from community organizations and fraternities are great choices when they meet school policy requirements. If there are ten males volunteering per grade level, the volunteers would be committing to only four days for the entire school year, which means that each male would volunteer one day every other month.

In the event a volunteer encounters a conflict in schedule, another volunteer could be contacted. The school counselor and/or school social worker could coordinate parental involvement in the school. The adult parent volunteers would help:

- Monitor students when they arrive at and leave school.
- Assist in hallways.
- Monitor bathrooms, locker breaks, and lunch periods.
- Assist with developing newsletters for parents and other communications.
- Monitor the classroom when needed for parent/teacher conferences.

Through parent volunteers, students would be able to develop bonds and relationships that would serve as a support network for them.

In addition, having parental involvement in the school provides students with additional adult supervision. After you get parents to volunteer in your school, create a climate of trust and openness. Be willing to hear and accept their ideas. Make every effort to make them feel welcome.

PARENTAL INVOLVEMENT

Although similar, parental involvement differs from parental responsibility. Parental involvement is the extent to which parents participate in every facet of their children's development from birth to adulthood. The ongoing involvement provides parents the opportunity to demonstrate their dedication and positive attention to child rearing. Through their involvement, they provide daily observation, support, stimulation, and encouragement, which may include activities such as:

- Reading
- Singing
- Making popcorn
- Playing catch
- Visiting the park for a child to play on playground equipment
- Touching, soothing, smiling, cuddling, and feeding
- Listening
- Attending school conferences
- Coaching, encouraging, and supporting
- Helping with homework
- Taking trips to the library
- Attending games and concerts
- Establishing quiet time
- Monitoring developmental progress
- Writing notes to the school
- Assigning chores
- Taking care of medical needs
- Volunteering in the school

These interactions of parents help promote normal child development.[5] In fact, many studies report that when parents engage children daily, the growth and the development of children are enhanced. Their physical development is promoted when parents provide nurture, love, support, and shelter. Their cognitive needs are met through a variety of experiences and opportunities for learning. Their social-emotional skills are advanced through modeling appropriate behavior that builds healthy relationships.

Obstacles to Parental Involvement

For some parents, although their intentions are to be involved in their child's development at school, their efforts are sabotaged by obstacles, which include:

- Work schedules
- Too many obligations
- Not enough time
- Their own discomfort about volunteering
- Children's difficult temperament
- Lack of emotional support from their partner

- Level of education
- Job responsibilities
- Belief that involvement is not needed
- Women employed outside the home because family living standards are increasingly dependent upon additional income
- Varied employment hours
- Inadequate parenting skills
- Several schedules to juggle
- Social pressures of society

When some parents are confronted with these obstacles, they believe they have insurmountable challenges. As a result, they develop pessimistic feelings about their lives and outlook for the future, neglecting to instill hope in their children. Then, if their perception is that they have a lifestyle without resources, they consider themselves powerless and incompetent.[6]

Their feelings of helplessness often cause constant turmoil and inconsistent parenting styles, which result in their children becoming confused. On the other hand, a situation of an enriching home life that is warm, safe, and friendly generates a healthy family structure. A healthy family environment is what guides children's success throughout life.[7]

When children's parents are fragile, the role of supportive significant others such as teachers, coaches, and ministers is important. As children need these support systems, their parents need them also. Support systems are especially critical when parents themselves do not know how to teach their children or where to seek tutoring or other available resources in the school or in the community.

SUMMARY

Educators, as you consider what love means in the school setting, would you agree that showing students you care is not difficult? In fact, showing students that you care is a great way to get to know them. This also allows you to get to know their parents, with whom you must partner.

Your understanding of students will help you better plan for their success. You will be able to earn their trust and respect. They will be motivated to work harder when they really want to give up.

Ask yourself, "Do I want to see motivation displayed in my students? Do I want to experience respect from them? Is parental involvement important to me?"

NOTES

1. J. Helper, "Social development of peers: The role of peers," *Social Work in Education* 19 no. 4 (1997): 243-54. Comer, 117-23.
2. Hergenhahn and Olson, 110-56.
3. P. Benson, J. Galbraith, P. Espeland, *What kids need to succeed*, (New York: Free Spirit Publishing, 1998).
4. R. Kirkshbaum, R. Dellabough, *Parent power*, (New York: Hyperion, 1998).
5. Durell, 108-76.
6. R. Herron, R. Burke, *Common sense parenting*, (Nebraska: Boys Town Press, 1996).
7. R. Weissbourd, *The vulnerable child*, (New York: Addison-Wesley Publishing Co., 1993).

Chapter Eight

Power

"In the main it will be found that a power over a man's support is a power over his will."
—Alexander Hamilton

Power connotes ability, strength, and exertion. When students are failing, they simply have no strength; therefore, they are less likely to be motivated to learn. Their feelings of unproductiveness provide no impetus for them to come to school or cooperate if they decide to come. When students are failing, if they come to school, they are more likely to cause problems in the classroom, impeding the learning of other students.

Then, if they perceive the actions of teachers as uncaring—having no interest in them passing their class—they will refuse to cooperate with their teachers. Uncaring actions derail student performance. Their responses will often include skipping classes, hiding in bathrooms, and leaving the school campus. To avert these behaviors of students, teachers' actions must reflect their awareness of students' needs and desires to experience success, which will afford them power. When teachers demonstrate caring, teachers strengthen students, resulting in students showing a greater interest in school.

Another way for teachers to strengthen students is develop activities in a manner that will allow students to master the skill. When teachers do this, they will see increases in the success of students. Greater success will be seen in students when teachers provide them with a working knowledge of assignments that facilitates accurate completion.

A simple way to do this is to consider children's learning style. Acknowledge that some students will require more time than others to master a skill. If many opportunities exist for each student to attain the needed skills, the likelihood increases for success.

TECHNIQUES FOR PROMOTING STUDENT SUCCESS

Numerous techniques must be considered by teachers in order to promote the success of students. Teachers must be willing to give quizzes in different ways. A suggestion is to give three quizzes and one test each month. Inform students of this. Then collaborate and coordinate with other teachers to plan not to give tests and quizzes on the same day that another teacher gives his or her tests or quizzes. Next, plan to give them on a specific day.

If a teacher gives his or her tests on Fridays, perhaps the first Friday of each month the quiz would be given orally. Every student would be expected to participate in the class discussion. This test score would be an automatic "A" for every student. This way every child experiences success.

The second Friday, the quiz would be given to each individual student, which would cover information from week one and week two. This quiz would help the student and teacher know what has been mastered. If further review was needed, the teacher and the student would be aware.

The third Friday, the quiz would be given allowing students to use their notes, which would cover information from weeks one, two, and three. This quiz would provide additional review and practice. In addition, this type of quiz would encourage note taking.

The fourth Friday, a test would be given covering all information for the four weeks. This test would allow students another opportunity to do well. It would also provide another opportunity for students to demonstrate what they gleaned from previous weeks of their class work.

Having reviewed for three weeks prior to taking the test, students would be better prepared. Adequate repetition would have occurred. Students would have had the opportunity for assimilation and accommodation, which are significant to their cognitive development.

Through their assimilation, they would be able to incorporate the new information taught into existing knowledge from previous lessons. Accommodation would be possible because the new information retrieved from previous lessons would have been adjusted. In addition, provisions would have been made for a greater understanding of concepts.

BENEFITS OF COLLABORATING AND COORDINATING

The power that students gain when teachers cooperate, collaborate, and coordinate their tests includes:

- It places students in a position that will increase their chances of doing well on their tests and quizzes.

- It increases the likelihood of students being better prepared for their tests and quizzes.
- It decreases feelings of powerlessness that emerge in students when given tests and quizzes on the same day.
- It reduces stress levels of students, knowing that they do not have to study for two or three tests that will be given on the same day.

Power is experienced when students are able to successfully complete their homework, which in some instances may require shortening homework assignments. This will allow students adequate time to do their own homework for all of their classes. They will have the opportunity to learn as they complete the assignment rather than meet a requirement and have no clear knowledge of what they have completed.

Extensive homework often serves to meet the requirement of the teacher rather than the need of the student. Extensive assignments often result in parents doing the work or helping with the homework. In this situation, the parent is concerned about the student meeting the requirement. The student then has no real power because the student has no knowledge of what he or she has completed, which is often indicative from his or her test scores.

If appropriate, teachers may give students an opportunity to have a grade dropped or to earn extra credit. After-school tutoring two days per week for reviewing and providing additional assistance for students needing it are other ways to help students. If feasible, teachers may suggest private one-on-one tutoring for some students.

To further foster the success of students, teachers may purposely allow repetition, giving a maximum of three different students the opportunity to respond to the same question during a class discussion. This would give students more than one example and promote their thinking and keep them engaged. Repetition would be helpful to attention deficit hyperactivity disorder (ADHD) and learning disability (LD) students who may need information repeated.

As mentioned earlier, note taking is another skill that teachers should encourage in students. Teachers should tell students that they need a composition book for their notes. Then, they should explain that each month the notes can be used when taking a quiz, which would help students make a good grade, which would increase their power.

Students must understand that knowledge affords them power. They must recognize that when they master a task, they have gained some power that will afford them the ability to move to another level. They must understand as they move to higher levels, their power increases, which often will provide them recognition.

For their accomplishments, they may gain social recognition, especially from their peers. Peers who do well tend to appreciate the hard work of other students. At school and at their church, certificates of achievement may be given to students. From this recognition student status is promoted, which generates power.

Their power is further escalated when they are promoted to the next grade. Passing the end-of-grade or end-of-course test is extremely important to students. When they are armed with knowledge in subject areas such as math, science, language arts, social studies, and reading, they make good grades and feel powerful. Their power heightens even more when they are allowed to lead.

Leadership offers students a chance to show off their skills. It provides them the opportunity to assist another student in solving, perhaps, a difficult math problem or in understanding the meaning of a concept. Through leadership, students are able to display their strengths.

Leadership provides a way for students to show respect. This is done when students model appropriate behavior. Their decisions will reflect responsible behavior.

IMPORTANCE OF TEACHER FEEDBACK

Teacher feedback on a regular basis is also critical to student power and achievement. Activities lack value when students do not understand them and the teacher provides no explanations or elaboration. Students will often show little to no interest or motivation when they do not understand concepts. Teacher refusal to explain and review information contributes further to students' failure and frustration.

In the classroom, if the teacher constantly models the skill and gives students practice time and presentation time, students will show some academic growth. The first two weeks of school should be used for activities that will allow the students and the teachers the opportunity to share experiences. The time used to get acquainted will prove essential for the overall achievement of all students and provide them with power to forge.

Another way that students experience power is working in groups. Initially, for the purpose of monitoring, grouping or pairing should be planned by the teacher. Teachers must make certain that students are not uneasy when approaching another student they do not know. After teachers observe this process for several days, the remaining days of the first ten days of school, students should be allowed to select two students they have teamed with previously.

The teacher will declare every team a "winning team," which will enable all students to feel successful and powerful. A slogan that the class might adopt is "Say It Loud, I'm Smart and I'm Proud." From this slogan, students may develop lyrics. The goal is to arm students with structured power.

A SENSE OF CONNECTION

As students are placed in groups, teachers will be able to identify the students who work well together and those who do not. Teachers will glean strengths of students as well as their weaknesses. The shy and fragile student will have a person to talk with and could possibly develop a friendship, which will likely eradicate cliques before they emerge.

The brave student will have someone with whom to share his or her stories. This form of grouping provides students the opportunity to connect and develop social relationship, which are crucial to their social development. Student grouping or pairing will prevent peer isolation and rejection.

It is often the child who is rejected who suffers in silence. Ostracism is uncomfortable and detrimental. Feelings of isolation can affect a student's aspiration, self-confidence, and motivation.

In addition, it is the unpopular child who is more likely to be a low achiever in school. Rejection often leads to adjustment and learning problems. Unlike the unpopular student, when a popular student exhibits inappropriate behavior, he or she is often perceived as having a "bad day." On the other hand, rejected students are rarely afforded tolerance.

A significant benefit of pairing or grouping students is that it helps students understand the concept of teamwork. Students learn that they must cooperate with their teammates if they want to get their projects completed. They further learn that cooperation in groups impacts their grades.

Along with cooperation, group work teaches responsibility. The outcome of projects requires that students be responsible for their portion of the assignment. When students are able to cooperate and be responsible in groups, they have mastered cooperative learning.

TECHNIQUES FOR FOSTERING LEARNING

To enhance learning, the teacher shows his or her commitment to helping every child succeed. The teacher demonstrates that no child will leave his or her class without experiencing success. In the classroom, the teacher states, "In this class we are a 'family' and in the 'family' we all work and learn together." The goal is to create an environment of acceptance and alleviate an environment of rejection, which causes some students not to be able to perform to their potential.

An excellent example of this is the experience of Benjamin Carson, a renowned neurosurgeon who was able to perform at his level of potential after acceptance. Initially, Dr. Carson was making failing grades and feeling rejected. One day, for the first time in his class, his teacher introduced a subject on which he was considered the "expert." Instead of being considered "dumb," Carson was perceived as "smart," and from that point, he became motivated and excelled.

In order for students to experience power, it is imperative for teachers to be committed to providing numerous opportunities for students to hear and practice what has been taught. Teachers can do this by introducing a new skill, then practicing the skill together with the students, and then allowing students to work together in groups. One group may model the task and then review the following day. At the end of each week or the beginning of each week, a short quiz could be given, reviewing what was covered.

As stated previously, the grade would serve to reveal students' acquisition of the skill and whether there is a need to reteach. For those satisfied with their grade on the quiz, they would not be expected to stay after school for tutoring. However, those needing help would be expected to stay for tutoring.

If students need transportation, then cooperation, collaboration, and coordination with parents and/or community agencies could arrange it. This approach would allow students' progress to be monitored weekly. It would also provide the opportunity to solicit parental input as appropriate. No parent should be surprised the last nine weeks of school with the possibility of his or her child being retained. Communication should be ongoing. If this is done, the likelihood for academic growth increases, which mirrors power.

To further promote student achievement, student input should also be obtained. Teachers should welcome the suggestions and comments of students relative to their learning needs. While the hard truths are not pleasant to hear, heeding them often improves the situation.

One way to obtain suggestions and comments from students is using a simple assessment tool at the end of each quarter. This will be a mechanism for asking critical questions that will improve student performance. The answers to the questions will allow teachers to make adjustments along the way.

Doing quarterly assessments would serve as a valuable tool for both the teacher and the student. It would provide the teacher with information about each student's individual need, and that will increase the likelihood of student success. Quarterly assessment would also serve as a vital tool for administrators. They could use it for accountability in terms of monitoring teachers' interventions in addressing the identified needs of students.

In addition to students, parents should be given the opportunity to provide written feedback quarterly. This would be a great way to solicit parental involvement and encourage communication. Both the parent input form and the assessment form could be as simplistic as illustrated on the next two pages.

QUARTERLY ASSESSMENT FORM

Teacher Name:
Student Name:
Subject:
This quarter, what did you like most about this class?
This quarter, what did you dislike most about this class?
To assist you in being more successful in this class, what would be most helpful to you?

QUARTERLY PARENTAL INPUT FORM

Teacher Name:
Student Name:
Subject:
What parental concerns, if any, do you have regarding your child's educational growth in my classroom?
What role would you like for me, the teacher, to assume regarding your concerns?
What role do you believe you need to assume regarding your concerns?

SUMMARY

When students experience power, they are motivated to learn. Instead of looking for ways to avoid school, they will come to school in hope of experiencing success. They will believe that they can learn and that the possibility exists for them to pass their grade.

Students will have hope because many opportunities will be in place to give them numerous chances to master various skills. They will start their week as a winner instead of a loser. The feedback from their teachers will provide them motivation and power. Their opportunity to give feedback will also produce power. And the comments of their parents that address their educational needs will contribute to the power they experience.

Educators, if you do this, do you believe you will help every student in your class experience some level of success? Do you believe that students will be more successful when quizzed in various ways? Do you believe it is overwhelming for some students to study for more than one test on a given night? Do you believe some students do not study at all because of feeling that it will be futile?

Chapter Nine

Fun

"A joy that's shared is a joy made double."
—John Ray

What makes learning fun is creativity. With creativity, students learn to brainstorm. Through brainstorming, students obtain ideas. Their ideas produce creativity.

Teachers provide creativity when they craft a learning environment that includes a variety of enjoyable activities for students. When children are happy, they will be more eager to learn. With numerous types of creative activities, students will find school an enjoyable place to be. When students are bored it makes it increasingly difficult for them to come to school.

To make math fun, an enjoyable technique that my child's teacher used to help the students learn inverse operations was a song. The class would sing the song to help them solve the equation. When taking their Algebra II test, they found that mentally singing the inverse song helped them remember the steps. To learn trinomials and other algebraic functions, the teacher taught the class a song, which helped improve their ability to learn.

The teacher's method of teaching showed students that they could learn in various ways. Using songs enabled the teacher to gain the students' attention and interest. The students found the activity fun; therefore, their teacher was able to engage them. A significant point about this method of teaching is it demonstrated that when various styles are used to teach, the learning style needs of students can be addressed.

Chapter 9
MAJOR LEARNING STYLES

Data widely support three major learning styles of individuals: auditory, visual, and kinesthetic. The auditory learner needs to hear and verbalize information in order to understand. His or her understanding increases when information is given with clear verbal explanations. These learners benefit even more from written decoded instructions and a quiet room without distractions.

The visual learner understands and remembers what he or she sees. This learner works effectively and productively with organization and order; therefore, a notebook to record daily assignments will enhance organizational skills. A variety of written materials of interest, including magazines, will foster reading.

The kinesthetic learner needs to hear, see, and perform in order to process information. He or she benefits from multisensory materials that allow touch learning because listening skills are weak. A variety of manipulatives will help stimulate this learner.

The learners' stimulation will further accrete when their parents are aware of their learning styles. Their parents must avert comparing one child to another. They must recognize that it is important for them to view each child as being unique, developing skills at his or her own pace. In addition, parents must avoid placing social and intellectual demands on their children that may be destructive.[1]

In another study of learning styles it was found that children who possess strong language skills were able to recite a story or poem after hearing it read only a few times. Children with musical talents were often able to pick out melodies by ear from the piano and from other instruments. Children possessing strong cognitive skills at an early age observed details, which enabled them to manipulate complex puzzles and draw images.

In this study, it was found that most children learned best in a quiet room. There were others who learned best in an open-ended learning environment. Then, there were some who required more structure, while others needed information presented in logical steps. Finally, there were some who were able to see the whole picture immediately, while others required additional time.[2]

TECHNIQUES FOR CREATIVITY

Creativity serves to enhance student performance. Students' ability to learn increases when educators provide an environment that offers creativity. A creative approach used to help my child learn how to subtract was a daily living skill. We used "real" dollar bills (something she could relate to), which increased her understanding.

After giving her five one-dollar bills and then taking away one dollar bill, she quickly learned that she only had four dollars left. This form of learning was meaningful; therefore, the concept was mastered expeditiously. She had no further problem with subtraction.

With division, we observed that she was omitting or missing numbers and getting lost in the process. To learn how to divide, each divisible was circled as she went through the process. By circling the numbers, she was able to master division successfully.

This is important because students cannot successfully do math if they miss a step or get lost in the process. They must be able to do step 1 correctly before they can move to step 2. When they cannot do this, they tend to become unmotivated and display little interest in their work.

PEER INTERACTION AND SOCIAL ACCEPTANCE

Students' interest will increase when they experience fun at school with their peers. They need social interaction and acceptance from their peers to promote their social development. The way this can be accomplished is to provide the opportunity for students to work with peers in the classroom.

As students interact with peers, they will learn how to develop relationships. Building relationships is important because it allows students to improve their social skills. Encounters with their peers create the possibility for acceptance. Once acceptance is gained, students are less likely to be alienated.

Assignments or projects create fun for students when they are associated with something to which they can relate. When given assignments or projects of interest that entail comparing and contrasting, children tend to gain a greater understanding. For example, an assignment of comparing and contrasting Romeo and Juliet with Chris Brown and Rhianna or Princess Diana and Dodi Fayed would likely be fun for students.

This assignment would help them organize events and facts. It will help bring meaning because students will have a greater understanding. They will be able to acquire critical thinking skills that help them sort fiction from nonfiction.

Most importantly, this assignment would prompt students to be more motivated to read about Romeo and Juliet. Their knowledge of Romeo and Juliet would increase, resulting in improved performance. Equally significant, their acquired knowledge would provide them self-confidence. Their confidence would help them develop a healthy outlook on life, which will motivate them to be productive because they have a sense of pride.

OBSERVATION OF MOTIVATION AND LEARNING

To make learning fun for a group of six exceptional children with severe behavioral and emotional disabilities, students were given an assignment with specific instructions but were allowed to have some input. A series of therapeutic group sessions were held with the behaviorally and emotionally disabled students who would not perform for their classroom special education teacher. After enthusiasm and motivation were developed in the students, they demonstrated their ability to learn.

The focus of the sessions was to get the students to use their time in their classroom constructively through writing. Each student was allowed to select a celebrity of his or her choice to write about. They were instructed and given time to find three resources to read pertaining to the celebrity. They were shown, using a graphic organizer, how to highlight significant facts. Then they formed an outline.

As they worked through the process, they wanted to demonstrate what they had learned by using their theatrical skills. After some discussion, it was decided that they could do some role-playing if they followed specific rules that the students and facilitator developed. The students made invitations and invited the administrator and their special education teacher to their performance.

Both the administrator and special education teacher were impressed with the performance and knowledge level of the students. The activity proved to be fun and it provided the students freedom to learn. Giving them some freedom to engage in a fun activity resulted in their being elated to show what they had learned.

When schools allow students to have fun, they will be more prone to come to school daily, fearing that they will miss an enjoyable activity. When students are having fun at school, they will be more likely to contribute to class discussions. The fun experienced by students will increase their participation, achievement, and attendance and thereby lower the student dropout rate.

SUMMARY

Engaging students increases their ability to learn. The best way to do this is to make learning fun. Students' interest is gained when learning is designed in such a way that students can see how it relates to daily living.

Students must understand the connection of concepts and abstracts. They must understand that there is a connection between the past and the present. Their understanding will increase when teachers use a variety of techniques to demonstrate.

Acknowledging that fun is important to students, would experimenting with something different, such as having a party the first fifteen minutes of school, reduce tardiness and prevent some student from missing class time? This does not mean you have to provide food each day, but when you do, collaborate and coordinate with a community partner such as a church, club, organization, or parents to donate the food. You may consider food once a month and not tell the students what day to expect food.

A suggestion requiring less planning, specifically for middle- and high-school students, is to give each student three points for every subject per grading period (nine weeks) if he or she is on time every day during the specific time frame of your class. This would be most effective if you shared this with your students when you review your expectations and grading rubrics with them. To involve them—get them invested—you may negotiate the possibility of earning two or three points (knowing that you have already decided on three points).

These points will contribute to their success and result in fewer tardy students. Imagine the number of students who will want to earn the points. Giving points would give some students the opportunity to change their grade from failing to passing, which is success!

Educators, consider this and also that knowledge is increased through a wide array of experiences. When schools provide fun activities for children, they will not want to miss school. In contrast, boredom will cause students to make attempts to avoid school. We know from our own experiences that people are more agreeable when they have input and are happy.

NOTES

1. M. Kappelman and P. Ackerman, *Between parent and school*, (New York: Dial Press, 1977).
2. C. J. Bellanti, K.L Bierman, "Disentangling the impact of low cognitive ability and inattention on social behavior and peer relationships," *Journal of Clinical Child Psychology*, 29 no. 1, (2000, March): 66-76.

Chapter Ten

Freedom

"Freedom is not merely a word or an abstract theory, but the most effective instrument for advancing the welfare of man."
—John F. Kennedy

The term *freedom* pertains to access. Freedom recognizes that every child has marketable skills. Children's performance is increased when given both responsibility and freedom within the classroom. They experience both when they have a voice in planning some activities in which they are expected to engage.

The expectation in schools is that teachers will introduce the activity. What is suggested is they provide some options that will be acceptable for students' selection. For example, teachers will give assignments but offer students the opportunity to complete it on Friday or Monday. Teachers may allow at least ten minutes daily for student/peer interaction in group activities, wherein the students are responsible to work quietly.

The freedom that students experience in their individual groups will help them learn how to work with others. They will discover ways to master tasks. They will even learn how to extrapolate from their own experiences to problem-solve and share ideas.

Students' experience in groups will provide a vital tool for review and the acquisition of creative ideas. They will learn how to talk among their peers and perhaps release some of their agonizing feelings. They will have freedom to express themselves in a constructive manner, which will help improve their social developmental skills.

Students who may otherwise experience rejection will likely gain a friend when given the freedom to interact with peers. The interaction provides a mechanism whereby constructive dialogue can occur among students. Freedom to interact with peers eradicates the possibilities of isolation and ostracism.[1]

As students are given freedom, their behavior alters. This change is not always chaotic. In fact, what has been personally observed in group sessions is that freedom serves as a viable means for children to be themselves.

The benefits of freedom strongly suggest that teachers should give students permission to take an active part in what they are teaching. Then listen to what students have to say. Some surprising and important feedback will likely be gleaned.

A PERSONAL OBSERVATION OF PEER INFLUENCE

From conducting a series of separate group sessions of female students and male students for a period of eight weeks, an impressive interaction among peers was personally observed. The sessions engaged ten male fourth-grade students and twelve female fourth-grade students in separate group sessions. At the onset, it was noted that females influence females and males influence males.

The primary purpose of the group sessions was to change student aberrant behavior. Among the female students, the targeted behavior was bullying (social isolation). Similarly, among the male students the main concern was teasing (verbal threats and hate language).

To invoke change in the behavior of the students, each student was paired with another student in the group of his or her choice. The role of the student was to influence positive behavior of his or her partner. In the sessions, the students were engaged in a variety of activities that provided opportunities for them to learn how to have a positive influence on their partner.

Their classroom teacher was included in this plan by using a behavior rating form to chart students' behavior weekly. The form was used to reflect whether appropriate behavior was observed most of the time, observed some of the time, or observed rarely. Incentives were provided weekly to the student with the highest overall rating and to the student most improved in each group session. Winners were given the opportunity to select a prize of their choice from a prize box.

The observations from the peer group sessions report were as follows:

- A female student had previously reported incidents of being rejected and ostracized and failing in all subject areas. This student had developed confidence in herself, made some friends, and was making passing grades in all subject areas.
- Another student who was an instigator, bullying and causing other students to be bullied, had discontinued bullying and had become a peacemaker, offering support to all the girls in her class.
- Another female student had gained social acceptance, and her grades had significantly improved.
- In the group of males, the teasing initially decreased then later ceased completely, resulting in fewer incidents of fights and suspensions.
- One male who had initially been reluctant to speak in the sessions began sharing his opinions.
- Another male who was stolid began to smile and speak whenever he saw this facilitator.

The rating form showed that every student's behavior improved. There was no significant difference between the male behavior and the female behavior. A negative that was observed from the rating form was that student positive behavior shifted when sessions were interrupted due to holidays and school breaks. Continuity created positive behavior, while intermitters engendered negative behavior.

This observation suggests that constructive dialogue is important not only in student and peer relations but also in student and teacher relations. Feedback from teachers makes a difference. Students, in most instances, want their teachers to listen to them. Therefore, whenever possible, teachers need to seek the suggestions of students.

One significant time when students' suggestions or feedback may be solicited is when classroom rules are developed. Before developing rules, teachers must clearly communicate that some rules are mandated while others may be formed with student input. For example, rules regarding dress code and discipline are not negotiable.

Some rules, such as eating, drinking, or chewing gum in class, may be at the discretion of an individual teacher. The problem with a rule of this type is that students tend to get in trouble in another class for what is acceptable in the previous teacher's class. Therefore, cooperation, collaboration, and coordination among teachers about what are acceptable rules would prevent this problem.

SUMMARY

Freedom matters. To mark this point, do you want to be totally restricted in how you teach? Students need freedom to learn their strengths and weaknesses. As they learn this, they will be able to make decisions that can enhance their learning. They will be able to share with their teachers what helps and what hampers.

Constructive dialogue will benefit both students and teachers. The shared feedback will help students know what they need to do differently, as it will teachers. Allowing students to respond respectfully will improve their social skills.

They will have a mechanism to be heard, which will encourage cooperation and eradicate frustration. As teachers listen, they will learn from their students. The information gleaned will be helpful in understanding the needs and situations of their students.

Given this, educators, will you consider that some freedom improves student performance? Do you believe you can develop ways for students to experience freedom in your classroom? And are you willing to allow your students to engage in constructive dialogue with you?

NOTE

1. Kittredge, K. "Today's youth face pressures from many unprecedented factors, not only peers" *Child and Adolescent Behavior* 16 no.6, (2000):1-4.

Chapter Eleven

Success for All

"Success is to be measured not so much by the position that one has reached in life, as the obstacles which he/she has overcome."
—Booker T. Washington

Educators, you, more than others, are charged with the task of educating children. And yes, many of you already do a lot to help students. The "Hook" does not require more of you; instead, it provides a way to make your job easier. If, from the outset, you offer love, power, fun, and freedom, I guarantee you that you will have fewer problems in your classroom and your students will be more successful.

One major benefit of the "Hook" is it costs absolutely nothing. It does not increase the school's budget or other expenses the school system has to manipulate. Another benefit is it is not complex. Applied properly, it will impact every child and thus close the achievement gap.

Now, imagine how you will use the "Hook" to elicit significant improvement in the academic performance of children. Next, consider that applying the "Hook" means acknowledging that human development is shaped by the environment. The environment plays a pivotal role in children's educational development and growth.

Applying the "Hook" also means that you, an educator, perceive family as being the most influential system in a child's life. You consider peers and community as resources that can positively shape children's development. You acknowledge that other environmental systems, including the microsystem, macrosystem, exosystem, mesosystem, and chronosystem, influence children's behavior.

Your acknowledgment and utilization of the "Hook" will generate "success for all," which includes students as well as educators. At every level, all students will experience academic success when they experience love, power, fun, and freedom within their developmental settings, especially within the school. At the elementary level, students will be less likely to feel uneasy about leaving home, a place perceived as warm and nurturing, when they experience love, power, fun, and freedom.

At the middle-school level, students will not have to experience continued ambivalent feelings about going to a new school, making new friends, and adjusting to changing classes when they experience love, power, fun, and freedom. This is important because middle school is considered the most difficult school years for students.[1]

Finally, at the high-school level, students will be able to concentrate better on meeting graduation requirements and preparing for college and or the workforce when they experience love, power, fun, and freedom. This is significant because high school is a trajectory of their life that is often overwhelming. Therefore, the "Hook" is crucial to their success.

The "Hook" provides a revitalized educational system that promotes love, power, fun, and freedom for all students, which increases the likelihood of:

- Eradicating fear
- Elevating motivation
- Improving school attendance
- Reducing dropout rates
- Escalating self-esteem
- Decreasing bullying
- Creating a positive self-image and a sense of self-worth
- Promoting academic excellence
- Producing pride
- Closing the achievement gap

Now, as a final consideration, administrators, teachers, and parents, embrace other challenges that will make a difference in student achievement. This means being courageous and examining yourself candidly. As you do this, you will become more aware of your own predispositions that function within and your own experiences that have guided the decisions you have made.

After you carefully do this, next ask, "Can I do more to improve the academic success of children? Should less time be spent looking for excuses and/or blaming parents and/or parents blaming teachers and administrators?" Be willing to look at the individual development of children with fresh eyes to better aid them in understanding their identity and making good decisions, which will help produce the desired changes needed to increase their performance.

Then, examine and/or reevaluate your belief, attitude, and practice regarding students.

Belief: Do you believe it is important for students to be able to connect one idea with another, which would bring meaning to learning and produce a greater understanding of the concept? If your answer is yes, ask yourself what you do to help bring meaning to learning for students.

Attitude: Do you present an attitude of care? If your answer is yes, ask yourself what you do to demonstrate care.

Practice: Do you provide ways for students or your child to be successful at school? If your answer yes, ask yourself what you do to help create academic success for students or your child.

Now, on the subsequent pages, read and respond to the specific challenges addressed to you.

ADDRESSING ADMINISTRATORS

Dear Administrators,

I tip my hat to you for aspiring to perform in such a vigorous capacity and doing the fine job that you do. I know some of the many challenges that you encounter. I also know that you make numerous sacrifices to perform at the highest level possible, addressing the needs of your school, especially those of students, parents, and your staff. Your dedication is appreciated.

Acknowledging that each day you receive far more concerns than you can possibly respond to, I strongly encourage utilizing every resource within your school to assist in addressing students' academic needs. Take time to consider what works well. Why? Look at what is not working. Why?

As you assess the challenges of your school, do not hesitate to consider the changes you may need to embrace to close the achievement gap. Parents and educators alike do appreciate your efforts. I especially thank you for your commitment and the role you play in positively shaping the lives of children.

Continue the good work that you do.

Challenges Posed to Administrators for Examination and/or Reevaluation Pertaining to Their Beliefs, Attitudes, and Practices

1. Is the present compulsory attendance law effective in improving attendance in your school?
2. Do you believe you are routinely evaluating the effectiveness of your teachers? How you are doing it?
3. Do you believe it is fair to students and their parents for the school to not communicate before there is a significant problem?
4. Do you believe your school offers programs that promote healthy peer relations?

5. Do you believe children feel safe in your school?
6. Do you believe students feel comfortable in a school where they are perceived negatively?
7. Do you believe your focus is on what is needed most for students to perform to their level of potential?
8. Do you believe the actions all of your teachers mirror what are considered those of a "good" teacher? If not, what are you doing to ensure that their performance improves?
9. Do you believe the students in your school are provided adequate grade-level transition assistance? If yes, what are you doing to ensure smooth transitions?
10. Do you believe social isolation impacts student performance? What do you do to address social isolation in your school?
11. Are you punishing children when you really do not clearly understand them?
12. Is your staff ill prepared to enhance student achievement?

ADDRESSING TEACHERS

Dear Teachers,

As a parent and an educator, I am very passionate about student success. Having spent more than twenty years in the public school system, I admire and applaud your hard work as well as every effort you have made to help children achieve academically. I have observed your struggles as well as your frustrations. I have observed your joy and your pain.

I concur that you should be paid more. In fact, it is ludicrous that there are insurmountable expectations of teachers, yet inadequate compensation. It should be recognized that it is the instruction of teachers that provides the foundation of every successful being.

In contrast, unfortunately, in many instances, it is the absence of the solid instruction of teachers that contributes to some unsuccessful beings. Therefore, in order to make a positive difference in the lives of children, I strongly encourage using the "Hook" and all your expertise in a manner that will close the achievement gap. All children will benefit as you apply and adjust the "Hook" to meet their individual needs.

Best wishes!

Challenges Posed to Teachers for Examination and/or Reevaluation Pertaining to Their Beliefs, Attitudes, and Practices

1. Do you believe you provide your students with a variety of learning techniques?
2. Do you believe you provide your students the opportunity to interact with their peers? What do you do?
3. Do you consider the resources of students when you give homework?
4. Do you consider students' learning style when you teach? How do you accommodate the various learning styles of students?
5. Do you make attempts to motivate all students to learn? What are the attempts you make?
6. Is your classroom environment conducive to learning, and do you believe it is fair to students and their parents when there is no communication from you prior to a significant problem?
7. Do you believe teacher traits influence students' adaptability, flexibility, and enthusiasm at school? What do you do to encourage adaptability, flexibility, and enthusiasm in students?
8. Do you believe classroom structure is important for student academic growth? What do you do in your classroom that provides structure?
9. Do you characterize low-income students as low performers? What are your reasons for this characterization?
10. Do you reduce academic expectations of low-income students? What is your reason for this decision?
11. Are you punishing children when you really do not understand them?
12. Are you ill prepared to enhance student achievement?

ADDRESSING PARENTS

Dear Parents,

As a parent, I appreciate and recognize your efforts in helping your child/children be successful. To further assist your child/children to work to his or her potential and excel, I urge you to be an ongoing advocate; never give up on your child/children. Make time to collaborate with and support your child's teachers. When it appears that you are fighting a losing battle, keep fighting. Eventually, you will see some positive changes.

I say this because I too have experienced some of the same difficulties with my child that you have with your child/children. I did not sit idle and watch my child fail when I knew great potential existed. Through consistent parental involvement, monitoring my child's academic progress, seeking tutoring beyond my ability to provide, and encouraging positive peer relationships, my child was able to soar.

A transition from not wanting to go to school to wanting to go to school, even when she was ill, emerged. Her poor academic performance and lack of motivation escalated to the point of believing it was "cool" to be smart, and she starting striving to make all "A's." In addition, the social skill deficits that she once displayed dissipated.

These changes did not happen overnight or without sacrifices and commitment on my part. Instead of accepting demanding positions such as administrator, professor, or director, I chose to remain in a job that would allow me to be more accessible to my child. Through my daily observation, her strengths and her weaknesses reflected a need for my personal involvement.

Parents, these are some of the reasons I know, if you do all you can to help your child, at some point you will see the fruits of your labor. I strongly suggest that you use the information in this book that will aid you in supporting your child's educational growth and development. You, as your child's first teacher, know best as to what is applicable in addressing your child's needs.

Best wishes to you and your children!

Challenges Posed to Parents for Examination and/or Reevaluation Pertaining to Their Beliefs, Attitudes, and Practices

1. Do you believe you can be more involved in your child's education? What do you need to do to be more involved?
2. Do you believe positive peer influence can be of benefit to your child? What do you need to do to promote positive peer relations?
3. Do you believe it is important for your child to come to school ready to learn? What do you do to make sure your child is prepared for school each day?
4. Do you believe children are confused by inconsistent messages? How do you communicate clear and concise messages?
5. Do you believe good health is essential to your child's well-being and academic success? What do you do to ensure that your child's health needs are met?
6. Do you believe a friendly home environment is a place where children can thrive? What do you do to provide a home environment that promotes healthy growth and development of your child?
7. Do you believe structure will benefit your child? What do you do to provide structure in the home to help your child experience academic success?

8. Do you believe that supervision and guidance are essential for the safety of your child/children? This also means keeping the school apprised of a current telephone number and an address for communicating with you. Your child may require emergency care. What do you do to provide supervision and guidance that will increase the safety of your child/children?
9. Do you believe your child should come to school with proper hygiene care? What do you do to ensure that your child does not have an offensive odor?
10. Do you believe it is important for your child/children to be respectful? What do you do to teach your child to respect other individuals?
11. Are you punishing your child when you really do not understand him or her?
12. Are you ill prepared to enhance your child's achievement?

NOTE

1. K. Jenning, *Federal education priorities and creating safe schools*. Assistant Deputy Secretary and Director of Office of Safe and Drug Free Schools in U.S. Department of Education (May 14, 2010).

Appendix

Getting Acquainted Form
(Teacher)
Name _____
School address _____
School number _____
Email address _____
University last attended _____
Number of years teaching _____
In my household, I have ___ children.
I have ____ brothers and ____ sisters.
For fun I like to _____. I like to _____ with my family.
The way I learn best is _____. What I do well is _____.
The person having the most influence on my life is _____.
My favorite food is _____.
My best friend is _____.
My favorite artist is _____.
My favorite athlete is _____.
The person I admire most (my hero) is _____.
My favorite place to vacation is _____.
My favorite holiday is _____.
Something significant I want you to know about me is that
_____.

Getting Acquainted Form
(Students)
Name _____
Father's name _____
Mother's name _____
Telephone number _____ Email address _____
Father's place of employment _____
Mother's place of employment _____
In my household, I have ___ brothers and ____ sisters.
My _____ and _____ also lives with me.
I have lived at my current address _____ years.
For fun I like to _____. I like to _____ with my family.
The way I learn best is _____. What I do well is _____.

The person having the most influence on my life is _____.
My favorite food is _____.
My best friend is_____.
My favorite artist is _____. My favorite athlete is _____.
The person I admire most (my hero) is _____.
My favorite place to vacation is _____.
My favorite holiday is _____.
Something significant I want you to know about me is that
_____.

Quarterly Assessment Form

This quarter, what did you like most about this class?

This quarter, what did you dislike most about this class?

To assist you in being more successful in this class, what would be most helpful?

Quarterly Parental Input Form

Teacher Name:
Student Name:
Subject:

What parental concerns, if any, do you have regarding your child's educational growth in my classroom?

What role would you like for me, the teacher, to assume regarding your concerns?

What role do you believe you need to assume regarding your concerns?

About the Author

Edwena B. Kirby, PhD, LPC is the author of *Shifting the Paradigm: Through the Lens of the Disadvantaged.* She is a child and family support team leader who has worked in the public school system, in low performing schools, for more than twenty years. She was trained at Yale Child Study Center in Comer's holistic school model that supports school and parent partnership. Her professional experience includes school social work, family therapy work, community college instructor, parent facilitator, instructor of the Parents as Teachers program, and supervisor of social service and mental health workers. She has served on various boards and has membership in many organizations that support the needs of children.

www.ingramcontent.com/pod-product-compliance
Lightning Source LLC
Chambersburg PA
CBHW030148240426
43672CB00005B/313